A CRASH COURSE

RELIGION

A CRASH COURSE

RELIGION

ADAM FORD

IVY PRESS

First published in the UK in 2019 by

Ivy Press

An imprint of The Quarto Group
The Old Brewery, 6 Blundell Street
London N7 9BH, United Kingdom
T (0)20 7700 6700 **F** (0)20 7700 8066
www.QuartoKnows.com

British Library Cataloguing-in-Publication Data
A catalogue record for this book is available
from the British Library

ISBN: 978-1-78240-873-4

This book was conceived, designed, and produced by

Ivy Press

58 West Street, Brighton BN1 2RA, United Kingdom

Publisher Susan Kelly
Editorial Director Tom Kitch
Art Director James Lawrence
Project Editor Caroline Earle
Design JC Lanaway
Illustrator Andrea Ucini
Design Manager Anna Stevens
Visual Concepts Paul Carslake
Series Concept Design Michael Whitehead

Printed in Malaysia

10 9 8 7 6 5 4 3 2 1

Dedication
I dedicate this work to my seven lovely grandchildren
with the hope and prayer that they should grow up in a
world which treats all faiths, and attempts to find
meaning in life, with respect.

INTRODUCTION   6

1 **MANY GODS & NO GOD IN ASIA**   12

2 **ONE GOD IN WESTERN FAITHS**   46

3 **CHINA, JAPAN & THE PACIFIC**   80

4 **AFRICA, AUSTRALIA & THE AMERICAS**   114

GLOSSARY   148
FURTHER READING   153
INDEX   156
ABOUT THE AUTHOR   159
ACKNOWLEDGMENTS   160

INTRODUCTION

Religions flourish everywhere around the planet, as they always have, shaping people's lives, providing meaning and spiritual guidance in a perplexing world, giving comfort in times of distress. They have a rich social dimension, holding like-minded people together in supportive groups, providing colorful calendars of high days and holidays that cycle throughout the year. And they usually tell a story about the world in which the individual feels they have a significant part to play: armed with their religious worldview, their lives make sense.

And yet, there is some unease in the twenty-first century about how to view religion: the violence of some religious extremists is seriously off-putting, while the increasing role of science as an explanatory force in our lives arouses the suspicion that all religion is delusional and out of date. Do we really in this modern era of science and technology need belief and faith systems that have their roots deep in what many consider to be fanciful storytelling and untestable claims about the nature of reality? A hard-headed scientific view of the world, however, cannot of itself tell us what to value or cherish, cannot answer all the questions we have about why we are here, or why our lives and those of other people matter.

A distracting thought arises when we note that there are so many different religions spread around the globe, each claiming to teach the truth. If you were born in southern Ireland, the chances are you are a Roman Catholic; if you were born in Vietnam then you will probably have grown up as a Buddhist, in Saudi Arabia as a Muslim—and so forth. These different traditions, with their various contradictions and differing claims, surely cannot all be right, we might think. They cancel each other out, all being equally misguided in their beliefs. Some believers, defending themselves, take an exclusive view of the truth, and claim that their own tradition is the only true one. Many retreat into fundamentalism and protect their faith from the apparent certainties of science, by claiming that their scriptures are literally and infallibly true, containing the unalterable words of God. This is the case with some branches of Christianity. Fundamentalists have taken to reading scripture in a way that denies other more nuanced interpretations made by past generations of believers, treating myths, for instance, as historical accounts of events rather than stories carrying inner meaning. Thus they insist on the historical accuracy of the Noah story: of a world flood unleashed on the whole planet by an angry God, rather than this being one variation of a multitude of local tales and legends recording worldwide memories of many different floods, at different times and different places. Fundamentalists' belief that the Genesis creation stories in the Bible are literally true has led them famously to deny all evidence of evolution on the planet, and the incredible age of the earth and universe, as revealed by science. They are forced to argue that God created the world, sun, moon, and stars roughly ten thousand years ago, scattering fossils in the ground to give a false impression of age.

The universal roots of religion

Notwithstanding the above concerns, a thorough and careful investigation of different religions opens up fascinating issues. The springs of religion that well up in the human heart and mind are universal, intrinsic to our very nature, essential perhaps to our well-being and spiritual health. They force us to explore some fundamental questions. We are conscious beings living in a vast universe—but why is there a universe at all? How are we to understand the astonishing miracle that has turned the material described in the periodic table of elements into creatures that ask questions? Do our lives have meaning beyond the daily concerns and anxieties about survival? How are we to judge between right and wrong, good and evil? How can we liberate the joy that may be latent within each of us? What is the best way to approach life's painful challenges, and what view should we take of death?

For all their differences it is these, and other, life-questions that are the concern of the various great religions. Contradictory answers abound—so, for example, the Creator God to whom Christians, Jews, and Muslims pray has no place in a spiritual tradition such as Buddhism. And when we die, are we reincarnated to live again in another body, as taught in Hinduism, or do we go to heaven—or maybe go nowhere, dead meaning dead? And yet, although they do not always agree on what is important, there can be a surprising amount of understanding between the various faiths and a shared sense of being on the same human quest. We may suspect that behind the contradictory dogmatic words there lies a deeper truth, a transcendent reality that generates a sense of the holy and the sacred. If we were to investigate, with an open mind, the different religion of a neighbor, we would very likely begin to respect their views, to discover that we have more in common than we expected, and to find our own faith being strengthened while learning from the other. In some urban centers, various communities of faith have found ways to come together to face a crisis, or to discuss challenges such as bringing up children in an inner-city environment—they even, despite their different backgrounds and beliefs, find that they can pray together.

We have to recognize that every religion has several dimensions that mean different things to different people. In the West it is often taken for granted that it is what you *believe* that matters: the doctrines of your church, which creed you recite. For many religious people, however, this is not the case; for them it is more the moral guidance they get, or the comforting experience of belonging to a group of like-minded worshippers, or sharing in the rituals and festivals of their religious year. Or it may be the teaching they receive that helps them find an inner experience of mindful peace, Buddhahood, or a sense of being at one with the natural world.

A geographical survey

In this crash course on religion I have adopted a geographical rather than historical approach, dividing the world into four areas. I begin with the ancient religions that emanate from the Indian subcontinent, such as Hinduism, Buddhism, and Jainism, to discover a whole spectrum of beliefs ranging from polytheism through monotheism to what might be called spiritual atheism. From there I turn to the Abrahamic faiths of the Jews, Christians, and Muslims of Arabia and Europe, with their belief in one God who speaks to them through their prophets. I also discover how a religion can break up into a rich variety of diverging traditions: Roman Catholics and Quakers, for example, are both Christian churches and yet show very few similarities. The third section looks at the way Indian religions found their way to China and Japan, mingling with equally ancient indigenous beliefs and practices, such as Taoism, Confucianism, and Shinto; I explore also some intriguing island cults of the Asia-Pacific. Finally, in the fourth section, I turn to the less well-documented tribal religions of Africa, Australasia, and the Americas, and look, as well, at three recent phenomena in the New World: the Mormons, Rastafarians, and Pentecostalists. I also consider the Aztecs, who developed a complex and in some respects horrifying religion allied to political power. Throughout the four sections the intention is to highlight the rich variety of forms that religion takes, recognizing the differences instead of pretending they are all fundamentally the same. Inevitably, with the space available, there have been some difficult decisions—what to include or leave out. I can only apologize if your favorite faith has somehow escaped attention.

There is a further question: what constitutes a religion? If dedication to a belief system is the mark of a religion, then we would have to include many "isms," such as atheism, or humanism, with its belief in human progress. Marxism, for example, has been described as a religion rather than simply a political philosophy, challenging the traditional Christianity of Europe (which it characterized as "the opium of the people") with its own prophet and founder, Karl Marx, and its own promise of a glorious future era, the rule of the proletariat replacing dreams of the kingdom of heaven. But sharing some features with religion does not make a belief system one. A way to sort out this sticky question is to consider whether a particular set of beliefs acknowledges there

is a spiritual dimension to life, pointing to something "other," whether it be the God of Abrahamic religion or the Not-God of Buddhism's Nirvana; do they have a sense of the transcendent, or experience of the sacred? Do the words "holy" or "numinous" have any place in their worldview?

Religions are not static entities; they are many-faceted, alive, and dynamic, evolving and changing with the times. One of the greatest forces for change builds up when people begin to feel dissatisfied with the established tradition, critical of its priests or leaders, doubtful of its teachings. This is precisely what happened in India, two and a half thousand years ago, when religion was dominated by a priestly Brahmin caste; the Buddha and others began to explore new paths for individuals to find their own spiritual way. Similarly, a protest movement against the corruption and control of the medieval Roman Catholic Church gathered strength in Europe, leading to a Reformation in religion, led by Martin Luther, Calvin, and others, and to the translation of the Bible into common tongues that made it available to the masses. Religions evolve and adapt depending on the needs and questions of their followers; they develop and grow old, as do people, empires, and flowers: some wither and die, such as Greek and Roman religions, from which only the names of their gods have survived. The Aztec religion imploded after the Spanish conquest in the sixteenth century.

The rejection of all religion

Some people, for various reasons, are opposed to all forms of religion, concluding that on the whole they are a bad thing and that the world would be better off without them. Most atheists hold this view—but we must be careful here, and remember that two thousand years ago the first Christians were accused of being atheists because they would not worship the gods of the Roman Empire. Atheism covers a wide range of differing beliefs. One person's atheism may be another's religion.

Two reasons for rejecting religious beliefs predominate. The first reason, as indicated earlier, has to do with the rise of science. It is assumed in this line of argument that humanity's religious thinking has evolved from magic and superstition, through animism and polytheism, to monotheism, finally to be superseded by scientism: science can now explain everything, denying religion its function. God did not design and make human beings, it is proposed—three billion years of random evolution created them. However, this ignores the fact that the majority of great scientists have been people with religious convictions and most believers welcome scientific insights into how the world was created, seeing God's hand in the unfolding laws of physics, chemistry, and biology. It also becomes apparent, from any investigation of religions, that providing an explanation for how we came to be here forms only a very small part of any religious tradition.

The second reason for rejecting religion is more troubling: its association with violence. Religious wars, the subjugation of women, the persecution and burning of heretics, fanaticism, terrorism—the list of horrors can seem endless. We all have to make our own judgments here: how much of the violence is a result of religious teaching and how much a consequence of human nature? It can be hard to disentangle these elements. Evidence from the twentieth century might suggest that human nature is the predominant problem; anti-religious totalitarian regimes created more sickening misery and death for tens of millions of fellow human beings than any religious power in history.

Religions come and go. Which will survive and why? Which present-day small cults will blossom into global faiths? Which can we trust, when it seems that some cult leaders and evangelists today are in it for the money or the satisfaction of an ego-trip? It is an old question raised over two and a half thousand years ago by the Jewish writers of the Bible. How do you distinguish a true from a false prophet? All we can do is look at their lifestyle and investigate their teachings. Do they have the ring of truth? Every religious movement must be examined for what it does for its members and how it affects those beyond its boundaries. Is it good for society as a whole? One of the unfortunate side effects of any religion is that while it provides followers with meaning in life and a sense of identity, these very attributes can generate a rejection of everyone else as being "them," or the "other." It can appeal to our deep-seated human tendency to be tribal.

A new threat now faces religious traditions, and one can only wonder which will survive the challenge. They may find themselves judged by the way they respond to the urgent demands of ecology. Nature has been forgiving in the past and the impact of humankind has been minimal. But our success as a species means that as our population increases we are overrunning the planet and devastating its ecosystems. How will each faith tradition face up to the threat that human behavior poses to the environment? Humankind is in real danger of destroying the natural world of which we are a part and on which we depend. We are polluting its atmosphere and its oceans, contributing to global warming, destroying the biodiversity of forests, spraying poisons indiscriminately over the landscape, all with little thought for the consequences for the next generation. Which religions have the necessary inner resources to respond with imagination, wisdom, and compassion to these immediate threats to the life of our home planet? It is a question they have to ask of themselves.

How to use this book

This book distills the current body of belief systems and religious practices into 52 manageable chunks, allowing you to choose whether to skim-read or delve in deeper. There are four chapters, each containing 13 topics, prefaced by a set of biographies of influential religious figures and an overview of key religious texts. An introduction to each chapter gives an overview of some of the main concepts you might need to navigate.

The Select Focus looks at one element of the main concept in more detail, to give another angle or enhance understanding.

Each topic has two paragraphs.

The Main Concept provides a subject overview.

Sentient beings are
numberless: I vow
to save them.
Passions are
inexhaustible: I vow
to extinguish them.
Dharmas are
immeasurable; I vow
to master them.
Buddha's truth is
incomparable; I vow
to attain it.

BODHISATTVA VOW

1

MANY GODS
& NO GOD
IN ASIA

ITRODUCTIO

The religions of the Indian subcontinent are so mixed and varied, so wide in their beliefs and non-beliefs, that they provide as colorful a spectrum of alternatives as can be found anywhere in the world.

Biodiversity of beliefs

The indigenous Indian religion Hinduism is ancient and without a named historical founder; it shelters such a complex and massively varied collection of beliefs and practices, gods and goddesses, philosophies and popular devotions, that it can be compared to the rich biodiversity of a forest. Like a natural forest it has grown, evolved, and changed over the millennia. Esoteric mysticism, for example, is able to flourish side by side with popular tree worship; while belief in a single Supreme Being, the One, sits happily with the colorful polytheism that covers Hindu temples with a pantheon of painted gods and divine animals. The origins of this great religious movement can be traced back four thousand years to the culture of Indo-Aryan invaders from southern Russia, the same people who invaded Europe at a similar time. The name Hindu is from a Persian word meaning river, having particular reference to the great River Indus (same root), which separated Persia and the West from the rest of the Indian subcontinent. Traditionally, however, Hindus have called their religion Sanatana Dharma in Sanskrit, roughly meaning the "eternal teaching" or "eternal religious order." The conquering Aryans quickly imposed their will on the indigenous peoples of India (Dravidians and others), absorbing some of the local gods and established rigid control of society through a pattern of social order called the caste system. For well over a thousand years the organization of religious practice was dominated by a Brahmin priesthood.

Rebirth and reincarnation

A common theme running throughout the various religions of India is belief in reincarnation: that death is followed by rebirth, each of us having experienced a multitude of lives as we are reborn again and again. Each individual is responsible for the way they live and is able to make spiritual progress through this chain of rebirths by building up a store of good *karma*. This belief offered hope to those born in the lower castes of society—perhaps next time they would be born higher up the social scale. Alongside this belief is a cyclical view of history holding that, as with individual lives, great eras of history come and go, experiencing birth, growth, and death, but through vast eons of deep time.

An individual path

A new individualism was emerging in northern India around 500 years BCE; cities were growing, partly fueled by the development of iron technology. Traditional patterns of rural society were being replaced in urban centers and the needs of individuals were changing. They yearned for something that was not being satisfied by the elaborate ceremonies and sacrifices of the priest-dominated system of the Brahmins. The Buddha, himself a city dweller, was alert to these needs and responded by developing a new radical way of understanding the world, offering a spiritual path for the individual: one that went beyond the popular gods of traditional Hinduism (but without denying them) and offered the possibility of finding inner peace in the ineffable state of Nirvana. Equally important and attractive was that the Path he taught was available to anyone, whatever their caste. The Buddha's teaching was so radical that he even gave up all ideas of there being a Creator God, and on these grounds some commentators have suggested that Buddhism is not really a religion at all but an atheist philosophy.

The same social unease produced another great revolutionary thinker in the days of the Buddha: Mahavira, founder of the Jain faith (which also dispenses with any concept of a divine creator), a religion known for its extreme respect for all life right down to the level of insects. The doctrine of *ahimsa*—"non-harming"— permeates Jainism's whole worldview and has even influenced some modern non-violent political movements, such as that of Mahatma Gandhi.

New faiths

While the Buddha and others were exploring new forms of spirituality, another religion was developing north-west of the River Indus: Zoroastrianism, which arose from the teachings of the prophet Zoroaster. A unique feature of this faith is that it viewed the world as the scene of a great conflict between the forces of good and evil. Later, in the seventh and eighth centuries, many followers of this religion fled into India from Muslim persecution, and came to be known as the Parsees ("Persians").

Finally, the sixteenth century saw the rise of Sikhism—an overtly monotheist faith founded by Guru Nanak, who aimed to reform religious society by making it casteless, open to everyone, and taking what he considered to be the best from Hinduism and Islam. His followers proudly defended this new religion by becoming effectively a military community when persecuted by the Mughal rulers of India.

BIOGRAPHIES

GURU NANAK (1469–1538)

Guru Nanak, the founder of Sikhism, was born a Hindu in the Punjab (present-day Nankana Sahib, Pakistan), although he leaned rather more to the simplicity of Islam in his teaching. He started adult life in the service of a Muslim official, but an inner restlessness made him quit his post, as he was much happier in the presence of yogis and other holy men. A religious experience transformed the direction of his life. When bathing one time, so the story goes, he disappeared. He did not return for three days, having been, in his words, "summoned to the Court of God" (possibly indicating a silent retreat in the forest). From then on he traveled widely, as a religious reformer, teaching men and women to find the Truth that lay behind Hindu and Muslim practice. He was influenced in his thinking by Kabir (1440–1518), a Muslim weaver from Benares who also claimed to have had a personal experience of the divine, referring to God in his poetry as the Beloved. Nanak, with his own songs, poems, and clarion calls for the Truth, attracted many followers, who came to be called Sikhs (meaning "disciples"). For the final years of his life, he lived as leader of a community on land given by a wealthy follower, and appointed Guru Lehna, whom he renamed Angad, as his successor.

THE BUDDHA (ca. 563/480–ca. 483/400 BCE)

The Buddha lived in northern India around the sixth century BCE (his dates are disputed) and is known by several names: Siddhartha Gautama, his personal name; Shakyamuni, meaning "sage from the tribe of Shakyas"; the bodhisattva, or "one who has vowed to achieve Enlightenment"; and the Buddha, meaning "The Enlightened One." Living the rich life of a Kshatriya warrior prince, he became dissatisfied with the luxuries surrounding him, particularly after a journey into town where he witnessed old age, disease, and death. Renouncing his pampered upbringing, and his family, he set off on a journey to find the truth about life. Time spent with various holy men led him to believe that the answer to his quest lay in the practice of asceticism and the denial of the body. For seven years he starved himself. Getting nowhere with these extreme austerities, he concluded that a Middle Way between luxury and self-denial was better. This freed him to practice yoga effectively and he achieved Enlightenment. The tree he sat beneath became famous as the Bo-tree, the Tree-of-Enlightenment, a recurring symbol in Buddhism. In response to this experience, he became a great teacher, attracting a large following of disciples, and founded a monastic order called the Sangha.

MAHATMA GANDHI (1869–1948)

Born into a Hindu family in Porbandar, in north-west India, Gandhi became one of the greatest social reformers of the twentieth century and leader of the successful independence movement against British rule. He went to Law School in London, then later practiced as a lawyer in South Africa where he encountered discrimination. It was there that, in 1914, he earned the honorific title Mahatma (Great Soul) for his work as a political activist, fighting for the civil rights of working-class Indians while developing his ideas of self-purification and Satyagraha (truth-force) with the use of non-violent protest. On returning to India he dressed in a simple white *dhoti*, always traveled third class on trains, fasted regularly, and practiced vegetarianism: he was quickly adopted by the masses as a holy man in the Hindu and Jain traditions, and became leader of the Indian National Congress party in 1921. Inspired by the Jain teaching of *ahimsa* (non-violence) he was able to see that "In a gentle way, you can shake the world." Gandhi's vision for India, on independence in 1947, was that it would become a nation of religious pluralism and tolerance in which Hindu, Muslim, and Sikh could live in harmony. Sadly this was not to be. He was assassinated in 1948 by a right-wing Hindu nationalist.

MOTHER TERESA (1910–97)

It is sometimes forgotten that Christianity is one of the oldest of India's religions, dating back to its introduction there in the first century CE. So, Mother Teresa, an Albanian-born Roman Catholic nun, was no interloper to the subcontinent when her religious calling took her to Kolkata (then known as Calcutta), in Bengal. She became well known internationally for dedicating her life to helping the poorest of the poor, founding the Missionaries for Charity in 1950. Her mission was to care for "the hungry, the naked, the homeless, the crippled, the blind, the lepers, all those people who feel unwanted." Her nuns follow this vocation in over 100 countries around the world. Always a controversial figure, she remained undeterred by criticism of her stand against abortion and divorce. She was canonized as Saint Teresa of Calcutta by Pope Francis in 2016, after two ostensible miracles attributed to her were confirmed by the Catholic Church.

SACRED TEXTS

THE *RIG VEDA* AND THE UPANISHADS

The *Rig Veda* is a collection of ancient hymns, divided into four sections, dating from a period between 1500 and 900 BCE, containing mantras and chants used by Aryan Brahmin priests in worship. Some were introduced to a new audience in the twentieth century by the composer Gustav Holst in his *Choral Hymns from the Rig Veda*. The word *Veda* comes from a Sanskrit word meaning "knowledge," and the hymns celebrate many gods, some of whom have since faded from the Hindu pantheon, such as Agni, god of fire (surviving in many European languages through derivatives of "ignis," the Latin for fire), and Indra, god of thunder. The Upanishads, more philosophical than the *Vedas*, were written down much later in around 800 BCE. There are well over 200 separate texts, of which a dozen or so are the most important; they contain a new emphasis upon Brahman (same word as the "Brahmin" priests but with a different meaning), the soul of the universe, the "One" hidden in all things rather as salt is found everywhere in the ocean. The discovery to be made by reciting the sacred syllable "Om," for example, is that the individual soul, the atman, is in fact identical with Brahman. This philosophy goes under the name of *advaita* ("not-two") and is summed up in the words *tat tuam asi* ("that art thou").

PALI CANON

The Pali canon is a large collection of Buddhist scriptures, about twice the length of the Christian Bible, deriving from the early Theravadin tradition. (The Theravadins or "elders" were later called the Hinayana—"smaller vehicle"—by their adversaries in the Mahayana "greater vehicle" tradition.) Pali was a dialect of Sanskrit, and the collection of writings emerged from early oral accounts of the Buddha's life and his teachings, finally written down in the first century BCE. These were recorded on palm leaves and tied together in bundles, the whole collection getting the name the *Tipitaka* (*Tripitaka* in Sanskrit), meaning the "three baskets," because of the way they were stored. One basket (*Vinaya Pitaka*) contained monastic rules for the community of monks, the Sangha; the second (*Sutta Pitaka*) contained stories about the Buddha, his disciples, and his sermons; the third (*Abhidhamma Pitaka*) is more philosophical, for advanced monks. Some disruption, repetition and lack of order in these early texts suggests that mice may have gnawed at the strings tying the palm leaves together, the three baskets having something of the nature of loose-leaf files.

THE ETHICAL CODE OF MANU: *MANUSMRITI*

The *Manusmriti* is the earliest ethical code in Hinduism, written texts of which date back perhaps to the second century BCE. Attributed to Manu, the legendary first law-giver, and supported by the myth that the caste system was originally created from the body of the God Brahma—the face (Brahmin priests), arms (Kshatriyas, the warriors), thighs (Vaisyas, the traders), and feet (Sudras, manual workers, pre-Aryan Indians)—it describes how people should behave in an ordered society. Manu's teaching recognizes the Hindu values of wealth (but not for its own sake), enjoyment, ethical merit, and spiritual liberation—*moksha*. The law code shows a mixture of concerns—including promoting veneration of the Vedanta, the religious philosophy of the Upanishads, and proper rules of religious sacrifice—while also spelling out how men and women should behave to one another, even going into details concerning a woman's property rights. The *Manusmriti* naturally reflects social norms of the era; so a woman is not allowed independence, because she is protected by her father when young, her husband in youth, and her sons in old age. Nevertheless, she is to be worshipped, as she is meant for bearing children, the good and light of a home. The *Manusmriti* further teaches that the night is meant for sleep and the day for work,

and that there are some great sins to be avoided, even by association: the murder of a Brahmin, drinking wine, stealing, and sexual intercourse with the wife of a teacher. Advice on old age reflects the tradition that at the end of life it was appropriate to give up all possessions and go on religious retreat. "When the householder observes wrinkles on his skin and white hair on his head, and sees also a son to his son, then he should take refuge in a forest" (6:2).

GURU GRANTH SAHIB

At a Sikh wedding a copy of the *Guru Granth Sahib* is the only witness necessary, such is the respect held for the holy book. It was the second guru, Angad, who, in the sixteenth century, first collected the Punjabi hymns of Guru Nanak and instructed that they should be written down. The collection of writings evolved and was added to by later gurus, who even included the teachings of Hindu saints and of two Muslim Sufis, until a definitive edition was produced by the tenth guru, Gobind Singh (1666–1708), who ordered that the scriptures, until then called the *Adi Granth* (First Collection), should be his successor and known as the *Guru Granth Sahib*.

HINDUISM

THE MAIN CONCEPT | Hinduism, with no named founder, established over the millennia a solid and integrated set of beliefs, with its *Rig Veda* and the Upanishads. The universe according to Hinduism is ancient and has experienced numerous cycles of history. The individual within this system experiences numberless lives through reincarnation, death being followed by rebirth. The link between lives is governed by the law of *karma*, according to which good or bad behavior, in thought, word, or deed, leads inevitably to rewards or punishments in the next life. The ultimate aim for many is to escape this round of rebirth into the liberated state of *moksha*. For many Hindus it is the worship, *bhakti*, of popular gods such as Vishnu and Shiva—the exploits of whom they read about in the two great Indian Sanskrit epics, the *Ramayana* and the *Mahabharata*—that dominates their faith. Such worship involves the burning of incense before their deities, and the lighting of devotional lamps fueled by ghee (clarified butter); religious processions carry the gods around towns and cities on highly decorated carts called juggernauts, while temple towers are covered in painted statues of gods and other heavenly beings. Other Hindus prefer a more mystical approach, and seek through meditation to become united with the soul of the universe, Brahman, of whom all the popular gods are deemed to be simply masks of that one deeper reality.

SELECT FOCUS | The image of the Hindu yogi, sitting cross-legged in the lotus position, and deep in meditation, is iconic. The purpose of yoga (meaning "yoked") is to be tied to a discipline of self-control, whether physical, *hatha yoga*, or mental, *raja yoga*. For some devotees it leads to the loss of the sense of self in mystical identification with the one Supreme Being, Brahman, soul of all things; while for others it leads to the loving worship, *bhakti*, of a god such as Vishnu or Shiva, the worshipper retaining their sense of their own identity. It is held to be essential not only to have a teacher, a guru, if one is to have any success with the self-discipline of yoga,

but also to practice in a quiet place away from distractions; on "a firm seat, not too high and not too low" instructs the *Bhagavad Gita*. Yoga cannot ignore the plight of others or be practiced while there is hatred in the heart; the yogi must have compassion toward all other beings.

SACRED TEXTS: THE *RIG VEDA* AND THE UPANISHADS
page 18

SACRED TEXTS: THE ETHICAL CODE OF MANU: *MANUSMRITI*
page 19

HINDU GODS
page 26

THE CASTE SYSTEM

THE MAIN CONCEPT | The four major castes in India, forming a rigid social hierarchy, can be traced back to early religious texts such as the *Mahabharata*. Some believed they were established by Brahma, the Hindu god of creation, though in fact they were imposed by the Aryan conquerors of India. The caste system is governed by the innate law of the universe known as dharma. The two top castes—the Brahmins, an elite priesthood, and the Kshatriyas, a ruling class of kings and warriors—believed themselves to be superior to everyone else (Aryan comes from a Sanskrit word meaning "noble"). Then come the Vaishyas—farmers, merchants, and artisans—and the Shudras: laborers. The Indian word for the four main castes is *varna*, meaning color, suggesting that the caste system has its roots in racial distinctions. A person's caste status was determined by birth, and marriage was only permitted within the caste group. At the bottom of the social system were some tribal people and the Dalits, the "outcastes," doomed to being street sweepers or latrine cleaners, "untouchable" by their betters. The major castes also break down into thousands of sub-castes or birth groups, known as Jatis. These groups are often separated by religious ideas of pollution, many refusing to share the same wells for drinking water.

SACRED TEXTS: THE ETHICAL CODE OF
MANU: *MANUSMRITI*
page 19

HINDUISM
page 20

THE *BHAGAVAD GITA* & KRISHNA
page 28

SELECT FOCUS | The plight of the "untouchables" was accepted as normal in Hinduism, a natural aspect of dharma, the law of the universe. Traditionally, and within living memory, if the shadow of an untouchable fell across a Brahmin in the street, the Brahmin was deemed to have been polluted and would need to return home to bathe and change their clothes. The only hope for these shunned lower classes was to "know their place" and, through working hard, to create good *karma* so as to be reborn into a higher caste in the next life. This lowly status of some people in society was mostly unquestioned as being the necessary price to pay for social good order, and was supported by religious beliefs. Things are changing, however, and the constitution of India, since independence, bans discrimination on the basis of caste, removing many barriers to social mobility. Today, many Dalits occupy powerful positions in government.

REINCARNATION & THE LAW OF *KARMA*

THE MAIN CONCEPT | Belief in reincarnation (which is sometimes referred to as the transmigration of souls or the doctrine of rebirth) is central to an understanding of the religions of India, Hinduism, Buddhism, and Jainism. It depends upon the assumption that the human soul (the atman) is eternal, wearing the physical body like a coat that is discarded at death to be replaced by a new body—human, animal, or even insect. The origins of the belief may lie in the observation of cycles in nature, such as death associated with winter being followed by new life in the spring. Some people claim that they can remember their previous lives; the popular *Jataka* tales in Buddhism are accounts of previous lives lived by the Buddha, recollected during the first watch of the historic night of his Enlightenment. The assumption in all traditions is that the atman is trapped in the rolling Wheel of Time (*Samsara*), each life being linked to the previous one by the law of *karma*. We are responsible for the blessings and curses that we experience in this life, because we created them by our behavior in our past lives. The aim of many religious disciplines is the release (*moksha*) of the soul from this cycle.

SELECT FOCUS | Belief in reincarnation (literally "to be made flesh again") reveals a very different view of time and creation than the one assumed in the Western Abrahamic faiths (Chapter 2, pages 46–79). Ancient Greek philosophers such as Pythagoras and Plato, believing in the eternal nature of the soul, took ideas of heavens and hells and rebirth on earth for granted. For example, Plato (fourth century BCE) wrote about it in "The Myth of Er" at the end of his most famous work *The Republic*. But, although entertained by some early theologians such as Origen (ca. 185–ca. 254 CE), belief in reincarnation was finally banned in Christianity as being heretical.

Also, as well as being hard to prove, reincarnation does not fit easily with the Judeo-Christian-Islamic idea of the individual as a unique and new creation by God with an exclusive once-in-a-lifetime chance of salvation and heaven. Christian creeds simply state a belief in "the resurrection of the body and the life of the world to come" as a hope of faith.

HINDUISM
page 20
THE CASTE SYSTEM
page 22

HINDU GODS

THE MAIN CONCEPT | How many gods there are in the polytheism of India is unknown. Some put it as high as 33 million, because every district and village has its own version of the divine—its own shrine, sacred tree, holy river, or revered goddess. Who you worship depends very much on local or family practice—and upon your own inclinations. Over time, the popularity and fame of some deities evolved, grew, and spread; Brahma, Vishnu, and Shiva are great examples. These three can be grouped as a trinity responsible for creating, sustaining, and destroying the universe, in that order. The grouping breaks down, however, if pressed too far, because each god is revered as the Supreme Being by its devotees: so in Vaishnavism (a major branch of Hinduism) it is Vishnu who is the power that directs everything that happens in the universe, demanding exclusive *bhakti* (worship). There are many goddesses, known as *shaktis*, in the Hindu pantheon, one of the most famous being Kali, wife of Shiva, who became a great, sometimes terrifying, power in her own right. For many Hindus, though, all these gods and goddesses are merely the faces behind which lies the One Ultimate Reality of Brahman, understood to be the underlying essence or divine life in everything. For the more philosophical or mystically minded, the religious task is to identify, through meditation, their own soul, the atman, with this ultimate reality.

HINDUISM
page 20

THE *BHAGAVAD GITA* & KRISHNA
page 28

SELECT FOCUS | Since the divine life runs through all things, there is no objection in Hinduism to portraying a god through the image of an animal. One of the most popular deities in India is the jolly-looking, pot-bellied, and elephant-headed god Ganesha, who grants success and prosperity to his devotees, being particularly helpful in removing obstacles in the way of merchant business. His statues usually portray him seated, with a large head and prominent trunk, sometimes with many arms; rats or mice may be shown around his feet, suggesting that he is also able to control the enemies of the farmer. Tradition has it that he was the son of Shiva and Parvati, that he lost his head in a family dispute, and that it was replaced with an elephant head by his mother. Hanuman, the colorful monkey-headed god, is another example of a popular animal deity.

THE *BHAGAVAD GITA* & KRISHNA

THE MAIN CONCEPT | The *Bhagavad Gita* (Song of the Lord), or *Gita* as it is more popularly known, has a place in the hearts of Hindus equivalent to that of the New Testament in Christian devotion. Written down roughly two thousand years ago as a small part of the great epic, the *Mahabharata*, it contains the essence of Hindu religious belief. Arjuna, a Kshatriya warrior, is in a moral fix arising from his caste status. The scene of the *Gita* is a battlefield where two armies, the Pandava and Kaurava, are readying themselves for war. Arjuna has relatives in both armies and is perplexed that his caste duty is to kill. Lord Krishna, an avatar of the god Vishnu, is his charioteer, and a dialogue ensues between them in which Arjuna learns about the inner battle his soul must fight. He needs to be detached and should be selfless in all his actions, fulfilling his duty as a warrior without any sense of fame or reward. Becoming aware of the immortality of his soul through his conversation with Krishna, Arjuna is overwhelmed by awe and filled with utter devotion for the Lord. After further dialogue, the warrior audaciously asks Krishna to reveal himself in his divine rather than human form. The vision is terrifying; in the light of a thousand suns Arjuna sees all things in God, the whole universe, all the gods, and all the destructions of time. He is overcome by awe and is greatly relieved when Krishna becomes an avatar once more, telling him, "Only by love can men see me, and know me."

SELECT FOCUS | The *Mahabharata* ("Great Indian Epic"), running to 100,000 verses in 18 books, is the longest epic poem in the world, the larger of the two great Sanskrit tales, the other being the *Ramayana*. While its authorship has traditionally been attributed to Vyasa, a revered and shadowy figure in Hindu storytelling, it is in fact a vast collection of stories about wars and marriages, gods and goddesses, religion, and caste duty, the roots of which lie deep in the past in ancient oral tradition. Dynastic struggles and family feuds, arson, and archery contests, dominate the tales, making the epic ripe for TV, film, or stage drama (Peter Brooks's 1985 stage version lasted nine hours). Embedded in the drama are eternal philosophical and religious questions about the paradoxes of life, and about death and immortality. So, for example, Yudhishthira, King of the Pandavas, a righteous man dedicated to virtuous living, ponders the devastation of a battlefield after the tragic horror of war, and the part that dharma (the Hindu concept of moral law) has had to play in this.

HINDUISM
page 20
HINDU GODS
page 26

THE INDIAN FLOOD STORY

THE MAIN CONCEPT | Many folk tales from around the world tell of a great destroying flood. In Hindu mythology, the first man, Manu, progenitor of all human beings, is warned of the coming deluge by one of the gods, who appears to him as an avatar in the form of a fish. There are various versions of the story in different texts, such as in the *Mahabharata*, or the even earlier *Satapatha Brahmana*; the god being either Vishnu or Brahma. A common theme is that Manu encounters a small fish when washing in a river and the fish begs him to protect it from bigger fish. Manu has compassion on the fish, popping it in a jar for safety, but it quickly outgrows this and has to be cared for in increasingly large bodies of water. One day the fish repays Manu's kindness by warning him of the coming flood and instructs him to build a boat, which he fills with animals, or, in some accounts, seven sages, who have salvaged the sacred *Rig Vedas* from the rising waters. They all survive as the boat finally comes to ground on a mountaintop. In Hindu mythology, the universal flood that destroys almost everything is but one episode in the great historical cycles of creation and destruction.

HINDUISM
page 20
HINDU GODS
page 26

SELECT FOCUS | Flood stories are ubiquitous, appearing among the legends and sacred texts of many religions. There is no evidence, or reason to think, that they all refer to a single universal flood; devastation caused variously by tsunami, storm, or broken natural dam would be enough to explain the range of traumatic tales. Nineteenth-century archeologists unearthed an ancient flood story in Mesopotamia in a text called *The Epic of Gilgamesh* that matched in its structure and detail the story of Noah in the Jewish and Christian Bible. In the Noah story God destroys the world because of humankind's sinfulness; in the Gilgamesh epic, Utnapishtim survives a flood sent by the gods because they were irritated with the noise people were making down on earth. Some stories ask the question "Why?"—trying to make sense of natural disasters—while others simply accept the unexpected flood as a tragic fact. The native Smith River people of California took the latter view and focused on the problem of rediscovering fire (which they achieved by traveling to the moon and stealing it from the moon people).

BUDDHISM

THE MAIN CONCEPT | The Buddha, who founded Buddhism in the sixth century BCE, grew up in Kapilavastu in northern India with the name Siddhartha Gautama, later taking the title Buddha, meaning the "Enlightened One." He was a religious revolutionary who rejected the priestly system of the Brahmins and instead analyzed life, rather as a physician will examine a patient. The Buddha summarized his diagnosis in the Four Noble Truths: all life involves *dukkha*, meaning suffering or "dis-ease"; *dukkha* is caused by craving and desire; the solution is to end the craving; and the method is to follow the Eightfold Path. The Eightfold Path, the heart of the Buddha's teaching, is all encompassing, covering every aspect of a follower's life—each of the following elements has to be *Samma*, "Right," and developed simultaneously: 1. Understanding, 2. Thought (together comprising Wisdom); 3. Speech, 4. Action, and 5. Livelihood (comprising Morality); and 6. Effort, 7. Mindfulness, 8. Concentration (comprising Meditation). There is nothing selfish about following the Buddha's path: it is not simply about personal salvation. Buddhist morality involves always practicing good behavior, never saying anything that might hurt someone else, and avoiding any form of livelihood that leads to the harm of another creature. It is a gentle, caring Way. The ultimate goal (and compassionate wish for others) is to achieve the selfless state of Nirvana.

SELECT FOCUS | The Buddha's diagnosis of life is as relevant today as it ever was. The temptation to cling to our problems, and to become absorbed in anxieties, is a natural human failing. The practice of Mindfulness, seventh element of the Eightfold Path, is designed to help with this and has become very popular recently in the West as a form of psychological therapy or general aid to conscious living. The aim is to cultivate awareness in the here and now, to wake up to how things are in the present moment, without allowing troublesome thoughts to disturb the calm. There is great simplicity in this: "When walking, just walk," said the Buddha; "when standing, stand; when sitting, sit; when lying down, lie down." There is a breathing exercise that trains this alert, wakeful, and untroubled state of attentiveness: it involves focusing on the incoming and outgoing breath while quietly acknowledging, then dismissing, disturbing thoughts.

BIOGRAPHIES: THE BUDDHA
page 16

THERAVADA & MAHAYANA BUDDHISM
page 34

PURE LAND BUDDHISM
page 92

ZEN
page 94

THERAVADA & MAHAYANA BUDDHISM

THE MAIN CONCEPT | Buddhism has always been a missionary religion, driven by compassion to bring spiritual guidance to all creatures; to release them from suffering and wrong thinking: it has spread all over the world from its origins in northern India. It developed and changed its form in a variety of sects, while always holding to the basic teachings of the Buddha. The earliest form of the faith, the Theravada ("the doctrine of the elders") has come to be known as the Hinayana ("the Lesser Vehicle"), and is still to be found in Myanmar and Sri Lanka: it offered an austere path favored by the Samgha, monastic communities, but was felt to be too demanding for lay followers. As Buddhism became popular it underwent an evolutionary change, and subsequent sects in Tibet, China, and Japan referred to themselves as the Mahayana ("the Greater Vehicle"). Many fundamental elements of the philosophy were retained, such as *anatta*—the teaching that the individuality of the soul is an illusion—or that the ultimate goal of meditation is the sublime state of Nirvana. But a new devotion to a multitude of Buddhas and bodhisattvas (great saints destined for Buddhahood) developed, fulfilling a need among devotees to worship and revere heavenly beings. The Buddha Amitabha ("infinite glory"), for example, was believed to have created the Pure Land of the West; while Maitreya, the future Buddha, waits in paradise to appear on earth when needed in troubled times.

SELECT FOCUS | One of the most famous of all the many Mahayana sutras (scriptures) is the Lotus of the True Law. It begins in the traditional way with the formulaic words, "Thus have I heard at one time . . ." establishing that the teaching can be traced back to the historical Buddha, even though it was written many hundreds of years after the Buddha's death. The word "phantasmagoria" has been used to describe the extraordinary content of this sutra, as it pays homage to a great multitude of Buddhas and bodhisattvas. The scene described in the sutra is of the Buddha addressing a vast crowd of *arhats* (holy men) and bodhisattvas, gods, goblins, demons, serpents, lay men and women; flowers rain down from heaven to celebrate the teaching. The sutra itself becomes a revered savior—anyone reading and learning from it, it is believed, will accumulate an immense amount of pious merit. Another text, the Diamond Sutra, has the great distinction of being the oldest block-printed work in the world, produced in China in 868 CE.

BIOGRAPHIES: THE BUDDHA
page 16
BUDDHISM
page 32

MARA THE EVIL ONE

THE MAIN CONCEPT | The equivalent of Satan in Buddhism is Mara the Evil One, but his role is far less significant and colorful than that of the Devil in Western literature. Heavens and hells certainly have a vivid place in Buddhist folk beliefs, often appearing in paintings on the walls of temples, illustrating the rewards or punishments that are earned through good and bad *karma*. They are not permanent states of being, but stages to be enjoyed or endured between death and rebirth. The hells reveal many torturing demons armed with knives and tongs and boiling oil, but Mara appears only a few times in Buddhist scriptures. His role is to distract the Buddha from achieving Enlightenment by clouding his mind with false views, and he is often represented by his daughters, who perform a lascivious dance to prevent the Buddha from discovering the peace of Nirvana. The daughters of Mara have telling names—Thirst, Discontent, and Desire—making it quite clear that they, and Mara too, are pictorial ways of presenting the difficulties faced in meditation. The Buddha was tempted by Mara to stay in Nirvana, but he rejected the idea and returned to the world out of compassion to give guidance to others.

BUDDHISM
page 32

YORUBA RELIGION
page 122

SELECT FOCUS | The enemy to Enlightenment throughout much of Indian spirituality, whether Buddhist or Hindu, is *avidya*, ignorance in all its guises—spiritual, physical, emotional, and intellectual—leading to craving, hate, and delusion. These three "poisons" are sometimes translated as Greed, Hatred, and Ignorance. Ignorance hangs like a fog over humanity, which is why the practice of right meditation is felt to be so important in following a religious path. The Buddha in his night of meditation beneath the Bo-tree experienced a clearing of the head and understanding of humanity's plight that led to his Enlightenment. The same truth is implied in Hinduism; in a famous image of "The Lord of the Dance" the Hindu god Shiva is shown ringed with fire, trampling on the demon Apasmara, who symbolizes ignorance. In Christian theology it is *sin* rather than ignorance that is the enemy, and Satan who is blamed for leading people into temptation.

JAINISM

THE MAIN CONCEPT | The founder of the Jain religion, Vardhamana, more popularly known as Mahavira (Great Hero), lived in the same century as the Buddha and, like him, was a member of the warrior caste, a Kshatriya, and not a Brahmin. He too promoted a revolutionary faith that was independent of the priestly Brahmin system. Jains claim, however, that Mahavira was simply the most recent in a long series of 24 great ascetics called *Jinas* (conquerors) stretching back through eons of time. Like the Buddha, Mahavira denied the existence of a supreme being (though not of other gods), believing in the eternity of individual souls, which are trapped in this world of *Samsara* (the endless round of rebirth) like flies trapped in jam. The aim in life should be to eliminate the bad *karma* that poisons the soul, with an emphasis on the practice of good works and asceticism rather than on meditation, thereby achieving *moksha*—freedom from the round of rebirth—and so liberating the spirit from the cloying world of matter. Jainism, unlike Buddhism, had no inner urge to "spread the word" through missionary activity and so remained a minority religion. It is best known for its doctrine of *ahimsa* (no-harm), which found its way into many peaceful political movements in the twentieth century such as that of Mahatma Gandhi in India and Martin Luther King in the USA, demonstrating to the world that non-violence is always the best way to conduct human affairs.

BIOGRAPHIES: MAHATMA GANDHI
page 17

BUDDHISM
page 32

SELECT FOCUS | Jainism is second to none in its respect for all living creatures. Jains feel compassion for all life forms, whether human, animal, or insect, believing that every living being has a soul, and that each soul is at a different stage in the migration of life from body to body through rebirth. The doctrine of *ahimsa* forbids Jains to "kill, ill-use, insult, torment, or persecute" any kind of creature. Their monks and nuns are known for gently brushing the path before them so as not to crush any tiny insect, and for drinking water through muslin to filter out any minute life forms. In this reverence for life, they bring to the fore a general feature of Indian religion: that is, belief in the sacredness of life, and the recognition that human beings are only part of an evolving process.

TRANSCENDENTAL MEDITATION

THE MAIN CONCEPT | In the 1960s, the practice of Transcendental Meditation (TM) became very popular in Europe and North America, attracting many celebrities such as the pop group The Beatles. The movement was led by Maharishi Mahesh Yogi, an Indian guru, with training sessions well advertised in the media and on posters. Over the following decades these training sessions were attended by millions worldwide, bringing calm and peace to many. The philosophy of TM is based on traditional Indian spirituality found in the Vedanta, although there is some debate about whether it can claim to be religious, because it is offered as being a secular and non-religious way of self-improvement. The attractiveness of the method lies in its simplicity; 20 minutes spent twice a day sitting in silence with eyes closed, reciting a mantra. A mantra is a personal word given to the student by the trainer, and repeated throughout meditation to bring the mind to a calm focus, making it easier to dismiss passing or troubling thoughts. One of the most famous is "*Om*," said to be the sound of reality.

SELECT FOCUS | The appeal of Indian forms of spirituality, meditation techniques from the Vedanta and Mindfulness practices from Buddhism, may have something to do with their "newness" for the Western mind; they come uncluttered with the doctrines of Christianity and offer a way for secular people to pursue a spiritual path without committing themselves to religious teachings they may have left behind. Many find Western ideas of God unhelpful, and reject doctrines of sin and guilt as religious templates that fail to fit their experience of life. Meditative prayer has always been part of the Christian tradition, however, and the use of rosaries—prayer beads—is a popular practice among millions of Roman Catholics. One of the earliest Christian mantras is the Aramaic *Maranatha*, "Come Lord": and the Jesus Prayer, "Lord Jesus Christ … have mercy on me," recited repetitively with one's breathing, has been used by Eastern Orthodox Christians since the sixth century.

HINDUISM
page 20
BUDDHISM
page 32

ZOROASTRIANISM

THE MAIN CONCEPT | The sacred scriptures of Zoroastrianism are the Avesta. The prophet Zoroaster (Zarathustra in Persian), who is generally considered to have lived in the sixth century BCE, roughly at the same time as the Buddha, was the religious reformer of an already ancient Persian tradition. Concepts of good and evil, and the eternal struggle between them, are central to his teaching. The God Ahura Mazda, Lord of wisdom and light, is at the heart of the faith, although he is opposed by a force of evil embodied in the figure of Ahriman, Lord of Darkness. The world is seen as the battleground in their struggle for supremacy—and even though Mazda is ultimately the winner, the religion is sometimes described as being dualistic; that is, divided into the two fundamental forces of good and evil. Ethics are central to Zarathustra's teaching, inspiring followers to take sides with Mazda and always to do good. Central to worship is the fire temple, because fire, a primary symbol of the religion, is considered to be pure. Zoroastrian funerals are distinctive in that they leave the corpses in high places, in "towers of silence," where they are exposed to the sky for the bones to be picked clean by vultures. Cremation is shunned because it would pollute the purity of fire.

SELECT FOCUS | A few Zoroastrians survive today in Iran, and in India where they are known as Parsees (meaning Persians), having fled there, seeking refuge from Muslim persecution, in the seventh and eighth centuries. They form a small, discreet, and prosperous community mostly around Mumbai, retaining high moral standards in private life and business, preserving the teaching of Zarathustra through the 17 hymns he wrote, the Gathas, and some of their traditional ceremonies. Unfortunately, owing to the indiscriminate use of pesticides on cattle, over 90 percent of India's vultures have recently been killed by eating poisoned carrion, and so the funeral method is being revised.

JUDAISM
page 54
CHRISTIANITY
page 58

Zoroastrian teachings have also survived in another way. Beliefs in angelic beings, heaven or hell after death (reincarnation is rejected), Judgment Day, and a powerful satanic-like force of evil, had great influence on the development of doctrine in the Christian tradition: the concepts came via Judaism, which was probably exposed to Persian ideas during the Babylonian Exile in the sixth century BCE.

SIKHISM

THE MAIN CONCEPT | Worship in a Sikh temple begins with the sentence "There is but one God whose name is true, the Creator," which sounds very like a Muslim statement. This is no random coincidence, because Sikhism was born in northern India, in the Punjab, where the two major religions Hinduism and Islam vied for supporters. Nanak, the first leader (guru), born a Hindu (1469–1538), later influenced by Islam, had not intended to found a new sect, but simply wanted to purify religion, and to effect a reconciliation between Hinduism and Islam, focusing on personal devotion to one God. In a famous utterance he said, "There is no Hindu and no Muslim." By the time of the fifth guru, Arjan (1581–1606), Sikhism had become a distinct and powerful movement, with the iconic Golden Temple at Amritsar glittering at the center of a vast water tank (pool). It is called the Harimandir—"the House of God"—and incorporates Hindu and Muslim motifs. It has four doors, indicating that it is open to men and women of all castes. With the tenth guru the line of leaders came to an end and the Sikh Holy Book, the *Guru Granth Sahib* (a collection of hymns and poems dating back to Nanak), became, along with the community itself, the principal authority of the religion. This sacred scripture is to be found lying open on a reading desk in every Gurdwara—the Sikh place of worship.

BIOGRAPHIES: GURU NANAK
page 16
SACRED TEXTS: *GURU GRANTH SAHIB*
page 19

SELECT FOCUS | Following their persecution under Mughal rulers of India, which sometimes led to martyrdom, Sikhs came to see themselves as a military brotherhood and, not wishing to hide their faith, proudly adopted the five "K"s to distinguish themselves from other religious groups. The hair was worn long and uncut (including a beard): the *kesh*. Unlike wild unkempt ascetics, however, the hair was to be washed, well groomed, and held together with a comb: the *kangha*. The *kirpan* (sword), marking dignity and self-respect in the face of oppression, may now be small and symbolic, but originally it was up to three feet long. The *kachs* are short pants worn by men and women, more practical in battle than the *dhoti*. Finally, there is the steel bracelet worn on the right wrist, the *kara*, signifying eternity, the oneness of God, Waheguru, the Wonderful Lord. The wearing of a distinctive turban, made from up to 16 feet (5 meters) of cloth and worn by all men, is of uncertain origin.

Whither shall I go then from thy Spirit: or whither shall I go then from thy presence?

If I climb up into heaven thou art there: if I go down to hell thou art there also.

THE BIBLE, PSALM 139:7–9

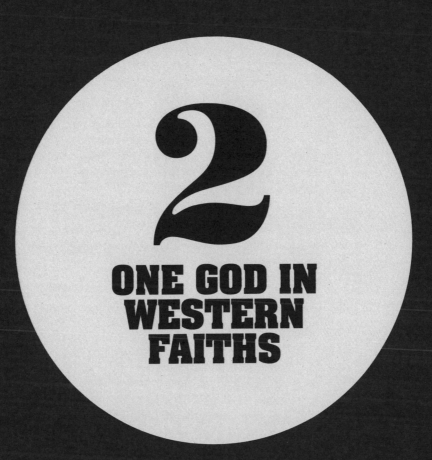

2

ONE GOD IN WESTERN FAITHS

INTRODUCTION

The three great Western monotheist religions—Judaism, Christianity, and Islam—are sometimes referred to as being Abrahamic; that is, growing from the same family tree of faith, tracing their belief in one God to "Father Abraham."

Father Abraham

According to oral traditions dating back to the second millennium BCE (actual dates being much disputed) and recorded in the Book of Genesis, Abraham is said to have lived in the city of Ur in the Chaldees, currently southern Iraq. He left his native land, believing himself to be instructed by God to do so, and traveled to Canaan, where he settled at Shechem. His conviction that he and his people had been chosen by God with a special mission to the world remained a central theme in later Hebrew and Jewish beliefs. For Christians he is held up as a great example of a man of faith obeying the will of God without question; Muslims count him as the first in the great line of prophets recorded in the Bible (including Jesus) and culminating in Mohammed, the "Last of the Prophets." Muslims also believe Abraham to be the ancestor of Arab nations via Ishmael, the son born to Hagar. Today, the tombs that are reputedly of Abraham and his first wife Sara are to be found near the West Bank city of Hebron.

Exile

A formative experience for the Israelites, the Hebrew descendants of Abraham, was when they lost their independence to the Babylonians and were taken into Exile in the sixth century BCE. For 70 years they lived as refugees in a foreign land, recollecting the time when their ancestors, in the days of Moses, were a slave people in Egypt. It was from this experience of suffering that the religion we now know as Judaism was born. Returning to Jerusalem, with tremendous hopes of rebuilding their nation and system of worship, they brought with them the new concept of synagogues (places of gathering for worship not dependent on a central Jerusalem Temple), and a collection of scriptures, the Tanakh ("Old Testament" in Christian terms), which had been collated and edited at this time. From then on they came to be called the Jews, taking their name from the territory around Jerusalem, Judah, originally occupied by one of the 12 tribes of Israel.

Further conquest by a foreign nation in 63 BCE, this time by Rome, created turbulent times and religious unrest among the Jews; expectations of a Messiah (someone anointed by God) who would restore the fortunes of the nation were stirred. Several characters laid claim to the role without success. Subsequently, Jesus of Nazareth—a prophet with powers of healing and a simple spiritual message that "The time is fulfilled and the kingdom of God is close at hand. Repent and believe the gospel (good news)"—emerged with a small band of disciples. His followers came to believe he was the promised Messiah, though this is not a title he seems to have claimed for himself. After a short three-year ministry, Jesus was crucified by the Roman authorities, giving rise to one of the most recognizable religious symbols the world has seen: the Cross. His followers carried his message eventually to the ends of the earth with the firm conviction that he had risen from the dead three days after his crucifixion. Called "Followers of the Way" (the Way of God), at first, those who followed Jesus only began to be referred to as Christians by their enemies in Antioch toward the end of the first century. In an extraordinary theological development, the Christian Church later came to the conclusion that Jesus was much more than a prophet—he was, they believed, the Son of God, God incarnate; the Word of God made flesh.

A new prophet

In the sixth century CE a new prophet arose in Arabia—Mohammed—who took exception to the idea that God had a son; "Only God is God," he announced. He also denounced the proliferation of popular minor gods in Mecca. Mohammed initially hoped that he would be recognized as a prophet by Christians and Jews, accepted as a reformer of the great tradition of the "People of the Book" (the Bible). When disappointed in this expectation, he changed the *qibla* (the direction of prayer) from Jerusalem to Mecca. In 622 CE Mohammed and his followers migrated from Mecca to Medina and established there the first Muslim community; the Islamic lunar calendar begins with this event: the Hijra.

Disagreements and disputes, in an all too human way, led to the disintegration of these three great religious traditions into the rich spectrum of groups, sects and sub-sects, churches and cults, orthodox and unorthodox, liberal and reformed, that we find today. This section will look at some of these—and at one valiant attempt in the nineteenth century, made by the Baha'i, to unite all religions in one.

BIOGRAPHIES

SAINT HILDEGARD OF BINGEN (1098–1179)

As a child Hildegard suffered much illness. Subject also to mystical visionary experiences, she joined a religious community of women when she was still young, attached to the male Benedictine monastery at Disibodenberg in Germany. Later, in 1150, she moved, with about 20 nuns, to an independent monastery in St. Rupertsberg, where she became abbess. It could be said she was a feminist before her time; Hildegard once famously observed, while pondering the biblical story of Adam and Eve, "Woman may be made from man but no man can be made without a woman." Her visions became a major influence in an extraordinary life and, following what she took to be a command from heaven, she wrote about them and their theological significance in a richly illuminated manuscript, the *Scivias*. One might assume that someone known for their mysticism and visionary experiences would have a tenuous hold on the real world: not so in the case of Saint Hildegard. She traveled widely, preaching throughout Germany, as the voluminous collection of her letters testifies. She invented a language, Lingua Ignota, with its own alphabet. She is also known for being one of the first natural scientists with a concern for medicine, and produced volumes of her own detailed observations of plants. In Hildegard's view God created everything in Nature to be of use to human beings; therefore there has to be a correspondence between what grows in the herb garden and holistic human health. Not content with these areas of expertise, this remarkable woman was also a very successful writer and composer, penning a morality play, *Ordo Virtutum* ("Play of the Virtues"), and a great quantity of liturgical music; recordings of her beautiful monophonic chants propelled her to fame in the 1980s. Although venerated as a saint by popular acclaim for centuries, Hildegard was not officially canonized until 2012, when Pope Benedict XVI declared her to be a Doctor of the Church.

THE VIRGIN MARY
(1ST CENTURY BCE)

Given the veneration and popularity of this Jewish woman over the last two thousand years, surprisingly little is known of the historical Mary, mother of Jesus Christ. Very quickly, however, the early church adopted her as a caring saint and she became adored as Theotocos, the Mother of God, able to intercede with her son in heaven when supplicants prayed to her with their requests. Legendary stories tell of her miraculous birth to Anne and Joachim (gloriously illustrated on the walls of the Scrovegni chapel in Padua by Giotto), leading to the belief that she was perfect, immaculate in her own right, clean of the universal taint of Original Sin. Thus, Mary provided a suitable womb and Immaculate Conception, through the power of the Holy Spirit, for the Son of God. Being sinless, she was thought not to be subject to death and so the doctrine developed that she was taken bodily into heaven, an event celebrated annually in Catholic churches as "The Assumption of the Blessed Virgin Mary" every August 15th. The cult of the Virgin Mary has become widespread on all continents, with gold-leafed statues and richly painted icons; many churches are dedicated to her name and local visions of her have inspired pilgrimages, such as to Lourdes in France, for healing. In some churches and chapels Mary may seem, to a visitor, to even outshine her son Jesus.

MOHAMMED (ca. 570–632 CE)

Mohammed was born in Mecca and orphaned at an early age; he became the great social and religious reformer of the Arabian Peninsula, revered today by almost two billion followers worldwide. Muslims are daily called to prayer with the words "God is most Great. I testify that only God is God, and Mohammed is His Prophet." When young, he was in charge of the business interests of his wealthy older wife Khadija and, although he later married several other women (Aisha, for example), his respect for her remained throughout his life, which may account for the reforms he introduced to improve the social status of women in his time, such as in relation to their inheritance rights. The significant religious experience that changed his life occurred in a cave when he was in solitary meditation on Mount Hira. God, he believed, spoke to him through the angel Jibreel (Gabriel) in a vision, commanding him to write; the Quran (the Recitation) was the result. During the rest of his life he received what he understood to be further revelations. He founded the first Muslim community at Medina in 622 and finally returned to Mecca, where he died in 632.

SACRED TEXTS

THE WISDOM OF BALAHVAR

Just as magnets attract iron, so religions attract elements from other traditions and incorporate them as their own. A good story is not allowed to go to waste. So it was with the very popular medieval tale of Barlaam and Josaphat, recorded in many languages in over 80 versions throughout Europe and the Middle East. This Christian legend tells of Barlaam—a wandering monk in a yellow robe—and a rich young prince who, dissatisfied with the luxuries and temptations of a transitory world, renounced them all in order to find the truth. These two were canonized in the Western Church and remembered on their Saints' Day, November 27th. It is only very recently that it come to be realized that the name Josaphat in medieval legend is a corruption of "bodhisattva," one of the titles of the Buddha—thus the Buddha had unwittingly become a Christian saint! The story has an intricate history but it can be traced back through Georgian versions to its Indian origins. Professor D. M. Lang translated and published in English one of these versions, "The Wisdom of Balahvar," in 1957.

THE BOOK OF PSALMS

For many Christian and Jewish believers it is the Psalms of the Old Testament that sustain their faith in God, whether read quietly in secret or heard being sung beautifully by a cathedral choir at evensong or chanted in a synagogue. Written down two and a half thousand years ago, they are very personal, straight from the heart, expressing anger and sorrow, joy and gratitude, in the certain conviction that they are heard, that the Lord is close by and listening. "Whither shall I go then from thy Spirit: or whither shall I go then from thy presence? If I climb up into heaven thou art there: if I go down to hell thou art there also" (Psalm 139:7–8). They record the anguish of particular events, such as the Exile of the Jewish people in Babylon in the sixth century BCE. "By the waters of Babylon we sat down and wept: when we remembered thee, O Zion" (Psalm 137:1). They celebrate joy, as when birds are found nesting in the Temple: "Yea, the sparrow hath found her an house, and the swallow a nest where she may lay her young" (Psalm 84:3). Remarkable voices from long ago.

THE NEW TESTAMENT

Unlike the Old Testament (the Tanakh), which contains material (myths, genealogies, histories, laws, psalms, and prophetic oracles) gathered over a period of a thousand years, the New Testament was written down and put together in the first century CE. It relates to the life of one man, Jesus Christ, and begins with the four Gospels (Matthew, Mark, Luke, and John—known as the four Evangelists), which are not biographies in the modern sense, but give an account of significant events in Jesus' ministry, focusing on his death and resurrection, his teaching, use of parables, and miracles. Matthew and John both knew Jesus, and Mark was a follower of St. Peter, one of the 12 original disciples. Luke was a companion of Paul, the early convert to the Christian Way. The Gospels are complemented by a collection of letters to local churches attributed to Paul, John, and Peter. Most of these derive from the Apostle Paul, and several were written before the four Gospel writers had gathered their material—in other words, within 15 years of the crucifixion of Jesus. Finally, the New Testament ends with the Book of Revelation—an extraordinary piece of apocalyptic writing by another John, known as St. John the Divine. It contains visions of Judgment, the End of Days, the Four Horsemen of the Apocalypse, and a New Jerusalem coming down out of heaven, sparkling with jewels and promising a grief-free eternity. It was composed during the cruel persecution of Christians by the Roman emperor Nero, who is identified by the cryptic number 666.

THE QURAN

Few scriptures are held in such respect by their devotees as the Quran. For Muslims it is the unaltered Word of God transmitted to the prophet Mohammed via the angel Gabriel over a period of about 20 years. The prophet (always rendered "Prophet," with a capital "P," by Muslims) did not himself write down the revelations he'd received, but they were memorized by followers and written down later on tablets, palm leaves, and bones of camels, finally to be collected together by Abu Bakr, the first Caliph. The acclaimed poetic beauty of the 114 *suras* (chapters) led to the development of a much-celebrated calligraphy: a principal art form of Arabic culture. The *sura* entitled "The Bee" invites the reader to consider the wonderful gift of honey that Allah gives to humankind. The *sura* "Mary" tells the story of the miraculous birth of the prophet Jesus. A recurrent theme is "Remember the days of Noah!" when Allah punished the sinful world with a great flood. We all face a day of judgment upon which our ultimate destiny will be decided: Paradise or Punishment.

JUDAISM

THE MAIN CONCEPT | At the heart of Judaism sits the family: lighting candles, drinking wine, eating together, and reciting traditional prayers in Hebrew on a Friday night in preparation for the Sabbath Day. Is it a religion, a racial identifier, or a culture (you are still Jewish if your mother is a Jew, even if you lapse from belief in the God of Abraham)? The answer is all three. To be a Jew is to have a strong sense of belonging to a special, chosen people; of being aware of the drama of ancestral history. Every year, at Passover, families gather together to remember how God, through Moses, led them to freedom from Egypt to their Promised Land. A thousand years later they escaped another period of bondage in a foreign land: Babylon. Today, these echoes from the past resonate with the horrendous experience of the Holocaust in Europe and the foundation, after almost two thousand years, of the State of Israel. Whether a Jew lives in Israel or is part of the Diaspora (the dispersion around the world), it is the family and Sabbath worship, with its readings in the synagogue from the Torah, that preserves the tradition. Like other religions, Judaism has divided into sects—in its case, Orthodox, Liberal, and Reformed—but the formative memories remain the same.

SELECT FOCUS | The Jewish Bible, the Tanakh, consists of three parts: the Torah, the Prophets, and Writings. The Torah, meaning the Law, is the most important of these; it contains the five books of Moses (Genesis, Exodus, Leviticus, Numbers, and Deuteronomy) and within these can be found the 613 rules that regulate orthodox Jewish life. Best known of these laws are the Ten Commandments —the Decalogue (Exodus 20)—which can be divided into three: those laws dealing with God (1–4); those covering relationships with other people (5–9); and one concerned with the inner life of the individual (10).

SACRED TEXTS: THE BOOK OF PSALMS
page 52
PROPHETS
page 56

1. You shall have no other gods.
2. Make no carved images for worship.
3. Never misuse God's name.
4. Keep the Sabbath Day holy.
5. Honor your father and mother.
6. You shall not kill.
7. You shall not commit adultery.
8. You shall not steal.
9. You shall not give false witness against a neighbor.
10. You shall not covet your neighbor's property.

PROPHETS

THE MAIN CONCEPT | It is a popular misconception that the role of a prophet is exclusively to foretell the future. Prophets figure prominently in all three Abrahamic religions, and are best understood to be interpreters of history, seeing the hand of God in all events, and commentators on public and private behavior. Inspired, they feel urged to speak for God, often critically, to their countrymen; their uncomfortable calling is to tell the truth, often despite opposition. Collections of their oracles make up a major part of the Old Testament: the Books of Ezekiel, Isaiah, Jeremiah, and a dozen so-called Minor Prophets. They proclaim judgment on neighboring nations that treat Israel badly, and on the people of Israel when they lose faith in God and return to worshipping at the altars of Canaanite gods. This theme was later taken up by the religious reformer Mohammed, founder of Islam, who condemned the worship of 365 gods in Mecca, even though it cost him support—in particular, when he rejected the worship of three very popular pagan goddesses, Allat, Uzzar, and Manat (initially permitted in the Quran in what came to be called "The Satanic Verses"). Christian writers in the New Testament quoted the prophets in support of their belief that Jesus Christ was the Messiah God anointed to bring healing to the world.

SELECT FOCUS | Many prophetic utterances, made in the name of God, concerned social justice—expressing the belief that God cares deeply for the poor and underprivileged. Minor Prophets such as Micah and Amos were critical of wealthy citizens exploiting the poor; of rich landowners seizing the fields of smaller creditors; of judges who, thrusting the rights of the oppressed to one side, could be bribed to make decisions in favor of the powerful; of traders in the marketplace who rigged the scales with fraudulent weights. Ostentatious religious practices, the prophets warned, mean nothing by themselves: "I hate, I scorn your festivals, I take no pleasure in your solemn assemblies," writes Amos (5:21).

JUDAISM
page 54
ISLAM
page 72

Micah was equally condemning of those who thought that making a show of religion exonerated them from criticism: "What does the Lord really want of you?" he asks. "To seek justice, practice kindness, and walk humbly with your God" (Micah 6:8). Many of these ideas concerning justice were developed in the nineteenth century by the promoters of socialism.

CHRISTIANITY

THE MAIN CONCEPT | Jesus was a Jew, as were his 12 disciples: they lived in Judea, a remote province of Rome, in the first century CE. From this small beginning there emanated what was to become the largest religion on the planet—Christianity—with over two billion followers today, divided into numerous major and minor sects. Jesus appeared as a prophet in Judea at about the age of 30, healing the sick and proclaiming a simple message: "The kingdom of heaven is at hand." Roman authorities saw him as a threat to their rule, and with the connivance of some local leaders had him crucified as a warning to others. His followers, who believed him to be the expected Messiah, became convinced that he rose from the dead three days later, an event celebrated today as Easter. Beliefs about Jesus quickly evolved, so that by the time St. John produced the fourth Gospel toward the end of the first century, he could write (John 1:1): "In the beginning was the Word, the Word was with God and the Word was God … and the Word was made flesh and dwelt among us." Two creeds, the Apostles' and the Nicene, later established this belief as orthodox Christian doctrine. Jesus, they stated, was God incarnate.

SELECT FOCUS | One of the earliest witnesses of the Jewish sect that was to become Christianity was Saul of Tarsus, later to be known as St. Paul. At first he was antagonistic to the new cult and tried to suppress it: but then, while on his way to Damascus to persecute followers of Jesus, he experienced a dramatic conversion (giving the English language a metaphor for all U-turns in belief; "The Road to Damascus") and became one of the most fervent voices proclaiming the Lordship of Jesus Christ. He was responsible for transforming the gospel into a message for all nations, welcoming non-Jews to the growing community of Christians. His letters to young churches form a major part of the New Testament; his first to the Corinthians contains the earliest account we have of Jesus' last supper, the origin of Christianity's celebration of Holy Communion (the Eucharist). His letter to the Romans lays the foundations for much of the Church's later theology.

CATHOLICISM
page 60

PROTESTANTISM
page 62

THE ORTHODOX CHURCHES
page 66

CATHOLICISM

THE MAIN CONCEPT | The Roman Catholic Church, the largest unified religious body in the world, traces its origins to a community already established in Rome by 50 CE. Tradition has it that its first bishop was the Apostle Peter, to whom Jesus is recorded to have said: "Thou art Peter, and on this rock will I build my church." This belief in the primacy of Peter, combined with the importance of the city in the Roman Empire, contributed to the church in Rome being seen as the mother church of all Christendom; Catholic means "universal," as used in the Christian Nicene Creed: "I believe in one Holy, Catholic, and Apostolic Church." Bishops of Rome are called Popes (from *papa*, Latin for Father) and were claimed in 1870 to be infallible in matters of doctrine. The hierarchy of the church, consisting of bishops, priests, and deacons, is all male, although communities of female nuns have an important role to play, as does the laity. The church feels responsible for proclaiming the gospel (good news) of God's saving action in the sacrificial death of his Son; and sees itself as the vehicle of God's grace, channeled through both its sacraments, and its clergy, in unbroken apostolic succession from Jesus Christ and the first apostles.

SELECT FOCUS | The sacraments are of central importance in the worship of Roman Catholic, Eastern Orthodox, Anglican, and various other churches, a sacrament being defined in the Anglican Book of Common Prayer as "an outward and visible sign of an inward and invisible grace." Ordinary water is sacramental when used in baptism, denoting the washing away of sin. Bread and wine are similarly so when used in the celebration of the Mass (otherwise called the Last Supper, Holy Communion, or the Eucharist), recollecting the words of Jesus: "This is my body" and "This is my blood"; they represent the body and blood of Christ, broken and shed at his death. Bitter disputes divided Protestants from Catholics about how to understand this sacrament, the latter believing that, in the Mass, the bread and wine change their substance into flesh and blood (transubstantiation); Protestants, on the other hand, tended to see them as a symbolic memorial. All traditions believe that by consuming these elements, the faithful share in the divine life of God.

BIOGRAPHIES: THE VIRGIN MARY
page 51

CHRISTIANITY
page 58

THE ORTHODOX CHURCHES
page 66

PROTESTANTISM

THE MAIN CONCEPT | A clue to understanding the nature of Protestantism lies in its name. It derived from a groundswell of protest in the sixteenth century against what was believed to be the medieval church's abandonment of early Christian teaching, coupled with corruption that accompanied the growth and power of church institutions (the sale of indulgences—remission of sins—being a particular example). Chief characteristics of early Protestantism are the acceptance of the Bible (and its need to be translated from Latin into local languages) as the only source of revealed truth; the universal priesthood of *all* believers; and the emphasis upon the fundamental importance of salvation through personal faith, a doctrine called "justification by faith." The individual Christian has direct access to God, it was believed, without the need for priests as intermediaries. Chief branches of Protestantism on the continent of Europe originally emerged from the teaching of the theologians who founded them—Calvinism (Jean Calvin), Lutheranism (Martin Luther), and Zwinglianism (Huldrych Zwingli)— but the emphasis upon personal interpretations of scripture led to many shades of doctrine and practice developing. Presbyterian, Baptist, and Lutheran churches today are happy to count themselves as being Protestant; the Anglican Church is less unified in this identification, preferring on the whole to see itself as a reformed Catholic Church—with Protestant elements.

SELECT FOCUS | The best-known name of the Protestant German Reformation is that of Martin Luther (1483–1546). He was a complex, melancholy, and pessimistic character, convinced of the sinfulness of all humanity and believing that no one can be saved by "good works"—"All we do is in vain" asserts one of his famous hymns—but must accept "justification by faith" alone in the saving action of God in Jesus Christ. This belief became the watchword of Protestantism. Luther emerged from the heart of the medieval church, at one time having been in charge of 11 Augustinian monasteries, but he made his name in 1517 by nailing 95 critical theses to the door of his local church in Wittenberg. He spread his views through pamphlets, condemning many Catholic practices and institutions: tributes paid to Rome, the celibacy of the clergy, masses for the dead, the doctrine of transubstantiation, religious orders, and the primacy of the Pope.

QUAKERS
page 68

BAPTISTS
page 70

PENTECOSTALISTS
page 144

ANGLICANISM

THE MAIN CONCEPT | The international Anglican Communion is a worldwide federation of Christian churches (third in size to the Roman Catholic and Eastern Orthodox Churches, with over 100 million adherents), which evolved from the Church of England (CofE), spreading through the British Empire and then into other countries—the map opposite highlights the various provinces of the Anglican Communion. The CofE, an episcopal (governed by bishops) church, emerged from the Protestant Reformation in the sixteenth century, treading a careful path between being catholic in its teachings, structure, and traditions, and protestant in its desire for reformation, while avoiding the extremes of Lutheranism and Calvinism. The monarch has been head of the CofE since the days of Henry VIII, when there was a break with Rome. The CofE sees itself as the reformed catholic church of the nation, tracing its traditions back to St. Augustine, the first Archbishop of Canterbury, appointed in 597 CE: the current archbishop is 105th in succession. Anglican churches around the world are held together by shared beliefs about the nature of the Church and by the 1662 Book of Common Prayer; their bishops meet every ten years in the Lambeth Conference, acknowledging the Archbishop of Canterbury (Primate of all England) as first among equals. Many member churches have recently carried the Reformation further and appointed female priests and bishops.

CATHOLICISM
page 60

PROTESTANTISM
page 62

SELECT FOCUS | The Book of Common Prayer (BCP) contains the English order of worship for Anglican churches, and includes Morning and Evening Prayer (amalgamating various pre-Reformation Latin offices), Holy Communion, Baptism, Matrimony, and other services. It also includes a lectionary (scriptural readings for the year) and 150 psalms from the Old Testament. The language, vocabulary, and masterly style had an immense influence upon the development of the English language, a debt that the Church and country owes to its original creator in 1549, Thomas Cranmer. Cranmer, as Archbishop of Canterbury, was instrumental in aiding King Henry VIII in the overthrow of papal (Roman) supremacy in the Church of England. He was later burned at the stake in 1556 during the reign of Queen Mary, a Roman Catholic. The final authoritative 1662 edition of the BCP was preceded by earlier editions in 1552 and 1559, as Catholic and Protestant wings of the Church argued about wording. It was revised in 1928.

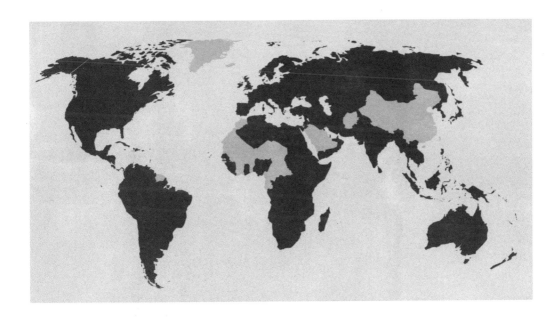

THE ORTHODOX CHURCHES

THE MAIN CONCEPT | The rift between the two great wings of Christianity—the Eastern Orthodox Churches (Greek, Russian, Coptic, Ethiopian, and many others) and the Western "Latin" Churches (Roman Catholic and Protestant)—can be traced back to the break-up of the Roman Empire. While retaining beliefs in the same creeds and accepting the fundamental teaching about Jesus as being the incarnation of God—Lord and Savior—they began to diverge on matters of political authority. The final schism can be dated from 1054, when the Patriarch of Constantinople (formally Byzantium) was excommunicated by the Bishop of Rome, the Pope, following a long-running dispute about a clause in the creed called the *filioque* (see opposite). The main act of worship in Eastern Orthodox Churches revolves around the Liturgy (literally "the work of the people"), the congregation mostly standing during a lengthy celebration of Jesus' last supper, which includes processions, incense, colorful vestments, and resonant chanting. It can be a deeply moving experience for the worshippers. An important element in their devotion is the use of icons, stylized and beautiful depictions of Jesus, Mary "Mother of God," and numerous saints. Despite concerns over idolatry, the use of icons as aids to worship, using eyes and imagination rather than words or written scriptures, has remained central to Orthodox spirituality.

SELECT FOCUS | The problem raised by the *filioque* clause that divides theologians of the Eastern Orthodox Churches from those in the West is rooted in the mysterious nature of God. If God is truly God, creator of all things from atoms to galaxies, then the nature of his inner being is thought by many to be beyond human knowledge or understanding. The Abrahamic faiths have always championed the idea that God is One—even Christianity, which also teaches that God is a Trinity; Three in One; Father, Son, and Holy Spirit. The doctrine of the Trinity is designed to safeguard belief in the oneness of God the Father, while acknowledging both the religious experience of Jesus' disciples that in knowing him they were encountering God, and the experience of the early church that God was known to them intimately as the Holy Spirit inspiring their minds and hearts. Eastern theologians denied that the Holy Spirit comes from both the Father "and the Son" (*filioque* in Latin)—maintaining that the Spirit comes only from the Father.

BIOGRAPHIES: THE VIRGIN MARY
page 51
CATHOLICISM
page 60

QUAKERS

THE MAIN CONCEPT | The Quakers, a Christian body otherwise known as The Society of Friends (of the Truth), were founded in 1668 by the Englishman George Fox when he drew up his "Rule for the Management of Meetings." He rejected church hierarchies, bishops, priests, sacraments, and all set forms of worship, preferring to be led by what Friends call the inner light of Jesus Christ. Quakers suffered some persecution at first, until the passing of the Toleration Act of 1689, by which time their fervent missionary work had led to the foundation of Pennsylvania in the USA, on Quaker principles, by William Penn in 1682. Their meetings, held in a plain, unadorned meeting house, begin in silence until someone feels an inner urge to speak, prompted, they believe, by the Spirit. Refusal of military service and any form of oath taking in court often brought them into conflict with civil authorities, but they gained respect for their emphasis on the importance of good works and for the moral character of their members, living lives of simplicity, purity, and truthfulness. Notable names include Elizabeth Fry, the great prison reformer; and Joseph Rowntree and George Cadbury, chocolate manufacturers with a moral grasp of capitalism.

CHRISTIANITY
page 58
PROTESTANTISM
page 62

SELECT FOCUS | Quakers recognize the need for Christians to take stock, regularly, of the spiritual health of their community and of themselves individually. To this end, a number of simple but searching questions have been developed since 1682, leading to the production of a small pamphlet entitled *Advices and Queries*, intended for use in Quaker meetings and in private devotion; any open-minded Christian, whatever their denomination, could find this publication a valuable basis for personal reflection. Quakers are thoroughly non-dogmatic, and the questions raised in the pamphlet all arise out of the basic belief that there is something of God in all of us, a truth that cannot be proved but that may be discovered to be true with experience. Questions that catch the eye relate to the natural world—"Are you concerned that man's increasing power over nature should not be used irresponsibly but with reverence for life . . . ?"—and to the state of society— "Are you working toward the removal of social injustices?"

BAPTISTS

THE MAIN CONCEPT | Baptists are one of the largest Protestant Christian churches, to be found worldwide with more than a hundred million members. They trace their origins to the inspiration of John Smyth, a Separatist who, having been ordained in the Church of England, broke with the tradition and went into exile in Amsterdam. In 1609 he reinstituted the baptism of adults rather than of infants—which scripture showed had been practiced in the early years of the Church—because a baby cannot profess either belief or repentance. This involves total immersion in water, preceded by a public profession of faith. It was part of the Protestant Reformation, aimed at returning to what were thought to be the practices of the early church, unadulterated by later tradition. Authority rests with the local congregation, each independent church relating loosely to other congregations; Baptists were always pioneers for freedom of conscience and religious liberty, and their ministers were called pastors rather than priests. In 1638 the first Baptist congregation was established in the USA, where today the largest grouping of Baptist churches—the Southern Baptist Convention—has over 17 million members. Baptists accept the mainstream teachings of Christianity, but tend to be more evangelical and missionary-minded than other denominations.

SELECT FOCUS | *The Pilgrim's Progress*, written in 1678 by Baptist preacher John Bunyan—a Puritan from Bedford, England—is the second-most influential religious book in English, after the Bible, having appeared in a vast number of editions and been translated into over two hundred languages. Bunyan presents his story as an allegory of the journey made by a Christian pilgrim "from this world to that which is to come delivered under the similitude of a dream." It is about the salvation of the soul. The pilgrim starts his journey in a truly Protestant way with only a Bible in hand; the pilgrimage he makes is an autobiography of the Baptist author's own inner life, with all its trials and tribulations. John Bunyan spent several years in Bedford jail, for no other offense than preaching without the authority of the established Church of England; when the reader encounters Giant Despair, the reference is more than obvious. The appeal of *Pilgrim's Progress* at the time of writing, and for long afterward, was immense.

CHRISTIANITY
page 58
PROTESTANTISM
page 62

ISLAM

THE MAIN CONCEPT | Islam (meaning "surrender," with Muslim denoting "one who surrenders"—i.e. to the will of God), traces its political ancestry to the merchant Abu Bakr, the first Caliph, who inherited authority from Mohammed, or to Mohammed's son-in-law, Ali. Muslims worship what they consider to be the same god as that of Christians and Jews, Allah simply meaning "The God" in Arabic. In the view of Muslims, Christians made the foolish and heretical mistake of worshipping Jesus, God's prophet, rather than focusing their veneration on the message itself. The Holy Quran is, for Muslims, the ultimate revelation from God; a scripture, not a person. Ever since their calendar began with the founding of the first Muslim community in 622 CE, all Muslims have been guided through life by the Quran; by a collection of Hadiths (stories about Mohammed and his sayings); and by *Sharia* law, including the five pillars of faith and duty; namely: 1. *shahada*: a declaration of faith that only God is God and Mohammed is His Prophet; 2. *salah*: prayer to be performed five times a day; 3. *zakat*: almsgiving, a percentage of one's wealth to be given in charity; 4. *sawm*: ritual fasting in the month of Ramadan; and 5. Hajj: the annual pilgrimage to Mecca.

SELECT FOCUS | *Sharia* law, practiced in Muslim countries, can be difficult to implement for Muslims living in non-Islamic lands, although some communities do set up their own *Sharia* courts to deal with family matters rather than criminal law. *Sharia*—an Arabic term—means "the path to follow," but has come to refer to justice in the community; it is based upon the Quran, and the Hadiths collected in the eighth and ninth centuries. Muslims, in their devotion to Mohammed as the ideal man, model their lives on his example, in everything from prayer, to what, or what not, to eat; washing; marriage and divorce; punishments for crime; business matters; and public disputes. There are inevitable disagreements about how *Sharia* law should be applied in the twenty-first century—for example, how much accommodation there should be with modern secular law relating to punishments for crime, or how to deal with the intricacies of international banking, with its dependency on usury (banned in *Sharia* law).

PROPHETS
page 56
SUNNI & SHI'A ISLAM
page 74
ISMAILISM
page 76

SUNNI & SHI'A ISLAM

THE MAIN CONCEPT | A schism formed in Islam at the very beginning, concerning who had inherited authority and power from Mohammed. A group formed around Mohammed's son-in-law Ali, married to Fatimah, the prophet's daughter, and was known as the Shi'a (party) of Ali. Numerous Hadiths supported his claim against the counter-claim of the major branch of Islam, the Sunni, led by Abu Bakr. Disputes between the two groups (not least because Fatimah had quarreled with Abu Bakr) led to civil war and, in particular, to the Battle of Karbala in 680 CE, which saw the death of Ali's younger son Husayn; from then on, Husayn was revered as a martyr, an impressive shrine being built for him, and he is remembered and mourned every year with great emotion on the anniversary of his death, the Day of Ashura, the tenth day of the Muslim month of Muharram. The Shi'ite community subdivided into a number of sects, the largest being the Twelvers, who accept the authority of the first 12 leaders of the Shi'ite community, known as Imams and believed to be the true successors of Mohammad, with political and spiritual power. They live with the expectation that the twelfth Imam, who mysteriously disappeared in the tenth century, will someday return as a messianic redeemer, the Mahdi. Today, Shi'ites are dominant in Iran, their leaders being called Ayatollahs.

SELECT FOCUS | The Sufis are the mystical wing of Islam, to be found principally within the Shi'ite tradition. They take their name from the word *suf*, meaning "wool," indicating their original simple ascetic clothing. For them it was not enough to be guided by the five pillars—they wanted a deep and intimate experience of God, to lose their own personalities in becoming one with God. This religious ecstasy (sometimes realized through dancing, as by the Whirling Dervishes) was justified, they believed, by Mohammed, who experienced a visionary ascent into heaven, which is celebrated yearly in the feast of the Miraj. However, Sufis often experienced persecution by Orthodox Islam. One of their great saints,

ISLAM
page 72
ISMAILISM
page 76

Hallaj, was executed for blasphemy by Muslim authorities in 922 CE for writing, among other things, "I am he whom I love, and he whom I love is I." Great names in this mystical tradition include the Andalusian Ibn Arabi (1165–1240); and Al Ghazzali (1059–1111), the most famous theologian of his day, who gave up his professorship in order to go and search for God, rather than being content simply to know *about* God.

ISMAILISM

THE MAIN CONCEPT | Ismailism, taking its name from Ismail ibn Jafar, an eighth-century Imam (spiritual leader), is a major branch of Shi'a Islam that broke away from the other leading Shi'a sect, the Twelvers. The Imams of the sect trace their ancestry to Fatimah, daughter of Mohammed. Aga Khan IV, the current leader of the Nazri Ismailis, the largest of the Ismaili denominations, is the 49th in succession. Found mostly in India in past centuries, the Nazri Ismailis have now spread around the world and number well over ten million, with impressive mosques in many major cities. Opposition from both Sunni Muslims and the Twelvers caused the Ismailis to become something of a secret society throughout the Middle Ages. Their doctrine of *Tawhid*, the oneness of God, is mystical, emphasizing his absolute transcendence, beyond space and time and beyond the words or imagination of human beings. To the five traditional pillars of Islam, they add two: purity, both physically, in the body and in hygiene of the home, and spiritually, in the heart; and *Jihad*, the struggle against inner personal failings, including, sometimes, the need for war to preserve social justice. Today, Ismailis' concern for human dignity is manifested in the foundation of many schools and hospitals.

SELECT FOCUS | An intriguing eleventh-century offshoot of the Ismailis, the Assassins became the subject of somewhat romantic legend and genuine fear. Embellished tales of these fanatical characters, dedicated to the purity of Islam, came to the West via Marco Polo. Their leader Hassan-i Sabbah, the mysterious "Old Man of the Mountain" who lived in a fortress in northern Persia, gave us the name "assassin" for trained killers; it is disputed whether this name derives from "hashish," which the Assassins were encouraged to smoke and so to dream of paradise before embarking on a mission, or from a Persian word referring to those who faithfully sacrificed their life to Allah, the *fidai*. They were a great and much-feared threat to the Abbasid Sunni authorities for a period of almost two hundred years, and were in their ascendency during the Christian crusades. Finally crushed by the Mongols, they have echoes today in the tactics of suicidal terrorists.

ISLAM
page 72
SUNNI & SHI'A ISLAM
page 74

T E BAHA'I FAIT

THE MAIN CONCEPT | The Baha'i faith (*Baha* possibly derived from Arabic, meaning "glory"), founded in Iran in 1863 by Bahá'u'lláh, is one of the youngest of the world religions, with over five million followers globally. It has the exalted aim of uniting all religious traditions, while also seeking unity among the peoples of the world; principles arising out of its belief in the essential unity of God. People of all races are encouraged to belong. The laudable aspiration for religious unity rests on the questionable assumption that all religions are variations of the same thing, all teaching the same truth. Originally, Baha'is emerged as a sect of Shi'a Islam, but their faith became an independent religion when they were persecuted as being heretical. Bab, a Persian predecessor of Bahá'u'lláh, had prophesied his coming, believing that Almighty God would send a messianic figure to bring spiritual truth to society, as he had in the past when sending the Buddha, Jesus, Mohammed, and many others. The collected writings of Bahá'u'lláh are believed to be revelations from God, and are as revered by Baha'is as the Quran is by Muslims. A nine-member central governing body of the Baha'is, named the Universal House of Justice, is elected by representatives from around the world, every five years; they meet at their headquarters in Haifa, Israel.

SELECT FOCUS | Bab (meaning the gate) was the title taken by Mirza Ali Mohammed when he first believed himself to be the one entrusted with preparing the world for the coming of a new manifestation of God, Bahá'u'lláh. As a young mullah (the title of one learned in theology and sacred law) in Shiraz, Iran, he believed that Islam needed a spiritual reformation and denounced the hypocrisy of other mullahs of his day. His belief that he himself was the divine Mahdi did not endear him to the orthodox authorities, but his championing of the poor, and critique of the status of women, won him many followers. The seclusion of women, he believed, was un-Islamic and simply a convenience for men. The remains of Bab, who was executed for apostasy (the deserting of orthodox religious belief), were removed from Iran and now reside in an impressive tomb in Haifa, near the headquarters of the Baha'i; they have become a site of religious pilgrimage.

SUNNI & SHI'A ISLAM
page 74

Without stirring
abroad, one can
know the whole
world;
Without looking out
of the window, one
can see the way
to heaven.
The further one goes,
the less one knows.

TAO TE CHING

3

CHINA, JAPAN & THE PACIFIC

I TRODUCTIO

Religious people in China and Japan are able to take elements from different traditions without fear of disloyalty or contradiction; they are eclectic. They do not share the inhibitions of the Abrahamic faiths Judaism, Christianity, and Islam, where each tradition, despite honoring the same God and tracing its faith back through the same prophets, tends to believe that its own worldview is the only true one and the others are false; and where a strong sense of exclusiveness is fostered with even greater rigor when it comes to other non-Abrahamic faiths, these sometimes being labeled as pagan or even evil. Compassion and understanding, of course, often overrule such inward-looking opinions, and the sense of exclusiveness can be softened. But in Chinese and Japanese religion there is no such problem. It is considered to be perfectly reasonable to follow a Confucian path through life, to be guided in spiritual matters by Taoism, and to employ Buddhist priests for your funeral rites. Mingling elements of belief and practice is deemed natural.

Confucianism and Taoism

Earliest forms of religion in China involved ancestor worship coupled with the veneration of nature spirits associated with agriculture; divination by means of oracle bones; and ceremonies to provide protection from evil spirits. The first writings appeared around the sixth century BCE with the scholar Kung Fu Tzu (551–479 BCE, his name being Latinized by Jesuit missionaries as Confucius), and Lao Tzu, the legendary founder of Taoism. Confucius was, for a time, a magistrate in Lu (now the province of Shandong), the state of his birth, where he taught a social philosophy attracting many disciples, who collected his sayings in a book called the *Analects*. His teachings stressed the importance of filial piety, respect for parents and elder brothers, and loyalty to the emperor. It was a conservative system that strengthened the status quo and it provided a structure of education for Chinese bureaucrats, right up to the early twentieth century. Some people have argued that Confucianism is not a religion at all, even though there are temples erected to the veneration of Master Kung. However, the fact that he believed in *Tien*, "The Will of Heaven" (a somewhat tenuous concept), and respected the value of ancestor worship, leads many to think otherwise.

Lao Tzu is a much vaguer figure and the book attributed to him was not written down until the third century BCE; the *Tao Te Ching* is a very beautiful work of mystical poetry advocating the simplicity of a nameless Way (the *Tao*) through life. Some of its thoughts chimed well with aspects of Buddhism when that Indian religion came to China, and the two traditions intermingled, Zen being one of the products.

The influence of Buddhism

Mahayana Buddhism appeared in China as early as the first century CE, the result of missionary-minded monks traveling east with their Sanskrit literature along trade routes, and Chinese cultural explorers venturing in the opposite direction. Some doctrines of Buddhism, such as reincarnation, were alien to Chinese thought, others attractive. Worship of the Buddha Amitabha by the Pure Land sect dovetailed neatly in the fifth century with Taoist dreams of a Western paradise of bliss. Salvation for devotees is by faith in the compassionate Amitabha Buddha. This notion of being able to depend on merit transferred from another person is central to the Buddhist ideal of the bodhisattva. Rather as some Christians may offer prayers for help to particular saints, so Buddhists believe they can gain merit from a bodhisattva, who has taken a vow to defer his own salvation, and final deliverance from the "great flood of suffering" in this world, in order to save other people. Relationships of Buddhists with Taoist and Confucian authorities were not always easy, but eventually Mahayana Buddhism became established as a Chinese religion.

Buddhism continued to travel east via Korea, finally reaching Japan in the sixth century when a number of sects took root there, one of the most well known being the meditation tradition of Zen. In Japan, Buddhists encountered, and learned to live alongside, the local and ancient Shinto, "The Way of the Gods." Shinto had no scriptures or organized religious tradition, or even writing; it was due to the competitive pressure exerted by Buddhism that Shinto's proponents came to write down their various colorful myths and legends in eighth-century chronicles called the *Kojiki* and the *Nihongi*. There are innumerable nature gods in Shinto, known as kami, and their worship at simple shrines celebrating aspects of nature and expressing gratitude to the gods is akin to the sort of religion to be found in Europe before the introduction of Christianity almost two millennia ago; and in some parts of India today. From Japan, the chapter moves further east to the islands of Melanesia and the South Pacific to consider some local indigenous cults that have developed in relative isolation.

BIOGRAPHIES

MA-TSU (b. 960 CE)

It was once said that "people become gods every day in China." Ma-tsu (a Fukienese word for grandma), also known as Tien-shang Sheng-mu (Holy mother of Heaven), provides a classic example of this process. The origins of her cult are obscure, but it is generally accepted that she was born in 960 CE on an island off the coast of Fukien province, her birth reportedly being attended by signs and portents. As a teenager she showed interest in Taoist mysticism and magic. It came to be locally believed that she had magic powers herself and used them to save her father and brother from drowning during a great storm at sea. She died young, but such was her fame that a temple dedicated to her was erected in her community. Stories of miracles proliferated and she was venerated as a guardian spirit, particularly by seagoing fishermen and other sailors. Two hundred years after her death, she became honored as a deity of national importance, a sea goddess to be worshipped all over China; in 1409 she was given the title "Imperial Concubine of Heaven," and later, in 1683, "Consort of Heaven," being recognized as a protector of the country, saving all by her great kindness.

MENCIUS (371–289 BCE)

Meng Ko, Latinized as Mencius, the most famous of later Confucian teachers, lived from 371 to 289 BCE. His teaching follows that of Confucius (which has been described as "humanism rooted in heaven"), and he stressed the importance of filial piety: showing respect to parents, even after their death. The moral life, he believed, follows directly from man's innate goodness reflecting the way of heaven: as water will not run uphill without being forced to, so evil actions are the result of a struggle against the true nature of a human being. The wise sage aligns his life with the way of heaven and so extends through society a transforming influence on others. Belief in the innate goodness of people was contested by some philosophers and Mencius sought to demonstrate its truth by posing a question about how an observer responds to seeing a child about to fall into a well—the immediate instinct, before any thoughts of rewards or fame cloud the action, is to save the child. While the *Book of Mencius* contains some mystical elements reminiscent of Taoism, Mencius is also known for teaching that man has the right to revolt against an unjust despot.

CHUANG TZU (ca. 369–286 BCE)

Chuang Tzu is a less shadowy figure than Lao Tzu. *The Book of Chuang Tzu* is much more speculative in its philosophy than the *Tao Te Ching*, asking interesting questions about the nature of reality. The author famously asked: "I dreamed last night that I was a butterfly—but how do I know, this morning, that I am not a butterfly dreaming that it is Chuang Tzu?" He believed that we should accommodate ourselves to living in a world of continual change, subject to the two formative principles of *yin* and *yang*. We should learn to accept, with equanimity, life and death, riches and poverty, success and failure, as they come—there is a touch of contented fatalism in this approach to conscious living. We should cultivate our inner spirit and, in so doing, nourish our lives with whatever experiences they may bring. When we have learned to live in accord with the course of Nature, we cannot be affected by sorrow or joy. This, said Chuang Tzu, is what the ancients called "release from bondage." Some of his thoughts are very Zen-like—he writes, for example, about the art of the master butcher, who can dismember an ox without hacking or false exertion, the blade slipping between the joints of meat with ease. It is in this unruffled manner (going with the flow of things) that we should learn to live our lives.

NICHIREN (1222–1282 CE)

Nichiren, son of a fisherman in south-east Japan, was ordained a Buddhist monk at the age of 15. He quickly became appalled at what he considered to be corruptions of the faith in many Buddhist groups, and later, at a conference of the 12 sects, he condemned them with the words, "The *nembutsu* (the mantra calling on Amida Buddha) is hell; the Zen are devils; Shingon is national ruin; and the Ritsu are traitors to the country." Such an intolerant attitude is unusual in Buddhism, and Nichiren was banished for a time. For him there was only one true faith, its final and perfect revelation being expounded in the Lotus Sutra by the eternal, cosmic Buddha, Sakyamuni (not the historical figure from India), and proclaimed in the mantra "*nam-myoho-renge-kyo*"—"Homage to the Lotus of the True Law."

SACRED TEXTS

THE *ANALECTS* OF CONFUCIUS

Confucius (551–479 BCE) made no claim to divine revelation, no pretense that he was inspired to speak for a god. All his teaching, recorded in the *Analects or Conversations of Confucius*, arose out of his concern for political and social good order; his thoughts were the result of hard work, not meditation (which he apparently tried but without success). The *Analects* are discourses written down, probably after his death, by the followers of two of his closest disciples, Tseng and Yu, who are referred to as philosophers in the opening paragraphs of the collection. The book was almost lost to the world in 213 BCE when the Emperor Ch'in Shih Huang ordered a great book-burning and the burial of scholars; he wanted to wipe out the past and for it to appear that history began with his reign. The emperor must have hated Confucius's admiration for rulers of the past and his continual reference to the wisdom of the ancients, about which he felt it his duty to teach and transmit. Fortunately, a few copies of the *Analects* survived. A thread running through all these conversations relates to the proper behavior of the superior man—and why the small-minded man should be shunned. The good moral character of rulers and others in high positions is particularly important, because

it will be infectious and will make the people good, rather as the "breeze bends the corn." At the same time, Confucius maintained, the people owe loyalty to those above them, although, as the Master said: "The wise man is intelligently, not blindly, loyal." Contemporary readers of these aphorisms and conversations quickly begin to feel themselves in the presence (after two and a half thousand years) of a cultured and wise gentleman, a man of good sense. There are also observations about Master Kung's own proper behavior, recording, for example, that he always fished with a line, never a net; and when shooting he never took aim at a sitting bird.

The concept of virtue runs throughout the *Analects*, and when asked to define this, Confucius replied that it involved the practice of courtesy, magnanimity, sincerity, earnestness, and kindness. Courtesy is a recurrent theme in his conversations, for it shows respect for the other person: one word that sums up a lifelong rule of conduct, he suggests, could be "sympathy." With sympathy you "Do not do to others what you would not like done to yourself"; the negative form of what has come to be called the Golden Rule, espoused by religious teachers in many other great religious traditions.

KOJIKI AND NIHONGI

The earliest records of Shintoism are to be found in two sets of scriptures written down in the eighth century CE; the *Kojiki*—"Records of Ancient Matters"—and the *Nihon Shoki*—"Japanese Chronicles" (usually referred to as the *Nihongi*). Writing had only recently been introduced from China in the fifth century, and it provided an opportunity to record many ancient myths that had survived thus far though oral tradition. These also served a political purpose in establishing the hereditary authority of certain families, particularly of the imperial clan and of Shinto priesthoods and shamans. The mythology they record begins with an eighth generation of gods (kami) named Izanagi and Izanami being instructed to make the world, which they accomplish by standing on the floating bridge of heaven and stirring the muddy chaos below with a spear. From the brine they make an island, to which they descend, make love, and give birth to the islands of Japan and to a multitude of gods (such as of wind, of trees, and of mountains). Izanagi, when purifying himself in a river, then created the sun goddess Amaterasu from his left eye, the Moon kami from his right eye, and the storm god Susanoo from his nose. There is subsequently tension between Amaterasu and her brother Susanoo, suggesting an agricultural background to these two most significant nature deities, the sun being life-giving while storms cause destruction. In the mythology, Susanoo antagonizes Amaterasu by destroying the rice fields, and tossing the dead carcass of an animal into her compound. Amaterasu, taking offense, retreats to a cave, where she hides herself. Eight hundred million kami, now plunged into darkness, gather outside the cave and implore the sun goddess to show her light. She is finally enticed out when a number of female kami do a torch-lit striptease act, causing uproarious laughter from the assembled throng. Curious, Amaterasu peeps out, only to catch a glimpse of herself in a mirror, which had been carefully placed outside the cave, and light returns to the world. The emperor's family traditionally trace their ancestry and power to this greatest of divinities, the sun goddess. And there are families in Japan today who also claim to be descendants of the kami who performed the risqué dance.

CONFUCIANISM

THE MAIN CONCEPT | The teaching of Confucius (551–479 BCE) has appealed historically to the natural human longing for structure and order in society, his system providing a conservative guide to both rulers and the ruled in China since the sixth century BCE. He accepted the value of ceremonies devoted to ancestor worship, because they strengthened family bonds, and to nature spirits, uniting farmers against the vagaries of nature. And he believed that his vision of society was in accord with the will of heaven, *Tien*; otherwise, he wrote nothing about religious matters, being more concerned with human virtue, his thoughts being collected later by students in the *Analects*. He was not a mystic like Lao Tzu, but a practical man with a strong sense of the importance of filial piety, advocating loyalty and respect for the emperor, of sons for their fathers, of wives for husbands, of younger sons for elder brothers. The superior man, he believed, should live a life of virtue, practicing courtesy, sympathy, and kindness. He edited, according to tradition, the Five Classics (see opposite), which became the core of Chinese education for mandarins. Confucius never claimed to be anything more than a teacher, but veneration by his followers has led to the building of temples in his name.

BIOGRAPHIES: MENCIUS
page 84

SACRED TEXTS: THE *ANALECTS* OF CONFUCIUS
page 86

FALUN GONG
page 106

SELECT FOCUS | Of the five Confucian classics it is the *I-Ching*, "The Book of Changes," that stands out through history; it is consulted as a book of divination both in eastern Asia and in Western culture, and is said to be the best-known Chinese book in the world. Today, it can even be consulted online. The ancient philosophy of *yin* and *yang* is implicit—that all events are subject to the two complementary conditions, weak and strong, wet and dry, female and male, earth and heaven, dark and light, and so forth. These are represented respectively by a broken line and an unbroken line. The lines are stacked in 64 groups of six, called hexagrams, which form the core of the *I-Ching*. When someone is seeking guidance from the book, randomly cast coins (or, traditionally, yarrow stalks) indicate which hexagram, with its own enigmatic oracle, is applicable to the question or problem in the mind of the consultant. Commentaries appended over the ages help the questioner interpret the result.

TAOISM

THE MAIN CONCEPT | It is sometimes claimed that Lao Tzu, who is acknowledged to be the founder of Taoism (*Tao* meaning The Way) lived at the same time as Confucius in the sixth century BCE, and that they met. Legend has it that this reclusive scholar retreated even further from the world and dictated the book associated with his name, the *Tao Te Ching*, to a local mandarin before disappearing west from China. Other scholars, however, question the whole legend and suggest that Lao Tzu (meaning "wise sage") is simply a title given to an anonymous author. Whatever the authorship, the *Tao Te Ching* (The Way and the Power) is a very beautiful piece of mystical poetry. It begins with the enigmatic line, "The Way that can be named is not the constant Way"; the Way lies beyond words and can only be known through simple living, going with the flow of life, like water, without thought of self, neither struggling nor striving. This way of living is called wu-wei, meaning "non-action," living quietly in harmony with nature. The implications for a ruler are simple—interfere with the state as little as possible; "Governing a large state is like boiling a small fish" (both can be spoiled by too much handling).

SELECT FOCUS | Taoism experienced a transformation in later years evolving into something rather different from its simple mystical past. The new focus was upon alchemy, divination, and the attempt to prolong life—even to find the secret of immortality. There are no gods, or God, in the *Tao Te Ching*, but as Taoism increased in popularity they began to appear, the Jade Emperor being one of the most distinctive. The religion diversified into many schools, while Taoist priests claimed the power to control evil spirits, to cure illness and disease, and to divert storms and floods. Many Taoist temples were destroyed during the Cultural Revolution of 1966–76, but there are still well over a thousand in China, with

PURE LAND BUDDHISM
page 92
FALUN GONG
page 106

attendant priests and nuns, and this ancient indigenous tradition is now experiencing a renaissance, supported by the authorities. Lay supporters seek harmony within themselves and in society by returning to the early mysticism of Lao Tzu, through simple living, sometimes vegetarianism, and charitable giving. There may be as many as 20 million followers worldwide.

PURE LAND BUDDHISM

THE MAIN CONCEPT | When Mahayana Buddhist travelers arrived in China from India (from the second century CE onward) it was with scriptures and colorful statues of Buddhas and bodhisattvas. One of the most popular of these was the celestial Buddha Amitabha (later "Amida" in Japanese), a divine figure, world savior, from the Pure Land (a Buddhist paradise), who had vowed to save every creature who calls on him with sincere faith and devotion. In iconography, Amitabha is portrayed in rich colors—reds, blues, and a great deal of gold; in paintings, he has a halo, with heaven or the sunset sky forming a background. Taoist priests identified the Pure Land with their own visions of a paradise which they located in the western sky, and so embraced the new religion with ease. Salvation rested not in the self-help of early Buddhism, but in the loving worship, *bhakti*, of this heavenly figure. A devotee merely had to recite his name to be saved. In Japan, the mantra "*Namu Amida Butsu*" (In the name of Amida Buddha), known as the *nembutsu*, is one of the most popular of holy invocations, chanted or whispered. The original idea of achieving Nirvana was not forgotten, however; by invoking Amitabha the devotee expects to join him in the Pure Land in the next life, from where it will be easier to attain final Enlightenment.

SELECT FOCUS | Buddhism never experienced the sort of internal problems presented by the adoration of religious images or statues that afflicted Christianity; they had no commandment forbidding the practice, no Protestant Oliver Cromwell (seventeenth century) to knock the heads off the statues of Catholic Saints, or modern ISIS extremist to blow up the ancient Buddha images of Afghanistan. Buddhists took the view, inherited from their Hindu background, that an image is simply a colorful representation of a divine being, a symbol of the truth that lies behind it, an aid to focus the mind until it is no longer needed. Important features in the iconography of a Buddha are the hand gestures, *mudras*. Amitabha is portrayed standing or sitting, one hand in the *mudra* of teaching and the other in that of meditation. The casual eye might confuse him with the original Buddha Sakyamuni—but the latter is distinguished by the "earth-touching" *mudra*, calling the earth to witness the vow he made in a previous life to attain Enlightenment.

BUDDHISM
page 32
BIOGRAPHIES: NICHIREN
page 85
TENRI-KYO
page 102

ZEN

THE MAIN CONCEPT | The word *zen* is the Japanese form of the Chinese term *ch'an*, meaning "meditation," which in turn comes from the Sanskrit *dhyana*. Tradition has it that this form of Buddhism was brought to China in the fifth century CE by a wandering monk called Bodhidharma; many images show him with piercing eyes and a thunderous expression. In the twelfth century it was introduced to Japan by a traveling Japanese monk, Eisai, from the already established Tendai school of Buddhism. The priority for Zen is achieving Enlightenment (*satori*) through meditation, which is claimed to be the true goal of original Buddhism. Zen rejected the popular notion that one can gain merit through devotion to Buddhas or bodhisattvas. At times it even went so far as the burning of scriptures and the rejection of images to make the point that Buddhahood can only be found within oneself through sudden *satori*. "If you ever meet the Buddha," goes one famous saying, "kill him." Zen is practiced by communities of monks living a simple life of work and sitting meditation (*zazen*). Enigmatic riddles called *koans* may be used to stall the mind and take it beyond discursive thinking to intuitive experience, (such as, "What is the sound of one hand clapping?").

BUDDHISM
page 32

BIOGRAPHIES: NICHIREN
page 85

PURE LAND BUDDHISM
page 92

SELECT FOCUS | Zen was introduced to the West in the late nineteenth century, some people suggesting that the first seeds were sown in 1893 at Chicago's "World Parliament of Religions." Since then, it has been popularized by writers such as D. T. Suzuki and Alan Watts (*The Way of Zen*, 1957). Its appeal stems from the simplicity of the way, its lack of doctrine, and the suggestive thought that each of us has the ability to achieve inner Enlightenment, if only we learn how to "go with the flow." Zen's influence on the arts in Japan, and on the free-flowing skills of the samurai warrior, added to the attraction. The way of Zen inspired beat poets such as Alan Ginsberg and Jack Kerouac, its ability to liberate creativity being enhanced by books with such appealing titles as *Zen and the Art of Archery* and *Zen in the Art of Flower Arrangement*. The Japanese 17-syllable poem, the *haiku*, became a popular way to explore experience, while the simplicity of the Zen-inspired Japanese garden, featuring rocks and raked gravel, attracted landscape gardeners.

CHINESE ANCESTOR WORSHIP

THE MAIN CONCEPT | It is probable that the earliest forms of religion worldwide involved ancestor worship, though this has become transformed or obliterated in many cultures. In Chinese folk religion the practice has not only survived but flourishes, fueled by respect for elders (a Confucian virtue), fear of ghosts, and the special veneration of particular individuals, elevating them to becoming local gods (in the West they would be re-labeled as saints). At the heart of the practice lies the universal question about what happens to each of us after death. In Chinese folk religion the belief is that the spirits of the dead exist in a nearby world; if they died in unhappy circumstances, such as drowning or by murder, they can cause trouble to family and neighbors, and need to be appeased through prayers and offerings. The majority enter the next world untroubled and, taking an active influential interest in family affairs, are grateful for being remembered, particularly on birthdays and at the annual Ching Ming Festival, when whole communities turn out to care for family graves and to picnic. Ancestors are often honored by the burning of paper replicas of things they might need in the next world, such as houses, cars, furniture, TV sets, and, most of all, money.

SELECT FOCUS | Many families manage to accommodate into ancestor worship the very different Buddhist beliefs in the afterlife. Doctrines of reincarnation and ancestor worship do not meld together easily and could even be seen as mutually contradictory—but folk religion seems to have no problem believing in both. Since it is believed in Mahayana Buddhism that there is a period, known as the Bardo, of 49 days between death and rebirth, many families adjust to this by removing the temporary family altar dedicated to the dead, after that time. The name of the dead person, inscribed on a wooden tablet that their spirit is believed to inhabit, is then housed in the small family shrine, where it is honored daily by the burning of incense sticks, and weekly or monthly by the offering of flowers, or vegetables in a bowl. After some years, when there is no one left who remembers a particular ancestor personally, the name tablet may be removed and stored with others in the local village temple.

THE BIRDMAN CULT OF EASTER ISLAND
page 110
YORUBA RELIGION
page 122

JAPANESE SHINTO

THE MAIN CONCEPT | Think about Shinto and your mind may conjure up images of the most beautiful cherry blossom in spring, or of that symmetrical iconic snow-capped peak, Mount Fuji. This is no accident. From earliest times Shinto ("The Way of the Gods") celebrated the natural world, acknowledged the sacred genius of a place, whether garden, lake, or mountain. It is a religion without scriptures or religious images and only needed to identify itself with the name "Shinto" when having to distinguish its "Way" from that of the new Buddhist Way introduced from China in the sixth century CE. There are many gods, known as kami in this popular and undogmatic religion; anything that inspires awe and wonder—rocks, waterfalls, or even people—may be called kami. Simple, wooden, thatch-roofed shrines are dedicated to the kami and attended by local priests, the emphasis in worship being on praise, cheerfulness, and gratitude. Bells are rung to summon the kami and sacred areas marked off with ropes. The most important of the deities is Amaterasu the sun goddess, who has the greatest shrine in Japan at Ise on the south coast, where her symbolic mirror is stored; the second-most revered shrine is that of her brother Susanoo, the storm god, at Izumo.

SELECT FOCUS | The iconic *Torii* arch (literally a "bird perch") associated with Shinto shrines, indicating the entrance to a sacred space, a gateway to holiness, is easily recognizable by those who have never even been to Japan. Often they are large enough for a road to pass beneath, and they have marked the presence of shrines for at least a thousand years. Very occasionally they may be found standing at the entrance to a Buddhist temple. Two pillars, traditionally made of wood or stone, carry a curving cross-beam lintel and, beneath that, a tie-beam; the whole structure is painted black and red and regularly renewed every few years. The *Torii* alerts the mind of the visitor, as they pass beneath the arch, to be prepared to encounter a numinous beauty in the view of a mountain or a grove of trees or the simplicity of a shrine. One of the most famous is the one-legged *Torii* of Nagasaki, which lost its second leg through the nuclear explosion there in 1945.

SACRED TEXTS: *KOJIKI* AND *NIHONGI*
page 87

DUAL SHINTO
page 100

TENRI-KYO
page 102

DUAL SHINTO

THE MAIN CONCEPT | Ryobu Shinto (Dual Shinto), with its ease of compromise, offered an intriguing and clever solution to the co-existence of different religions. As soon as some of the major schools of Buddhism—the Tendai and Shingon—became established in Japan, the question arose about how to accommodate the various Buddhas and bodhisattvas of the Mahayana tradition with the many deities of Shinto. By the eighth century a solution was found. Shinto's natural syncretism and Buddhism's ability to tolerate other beliefs made it a very simple matter to identify Shinto gods with Buddhas and bodhisattvas, and vice versa. It could then be believed that the Mahayana Buddha Vairocana had, out of compassion, manifested himself to the Japanese as the sun goddess Amaterasu in order to bring them closer to Buddhahood. On the whole, the immigrant Buddhist tradition took control of the situation and Buddhist temples and images were set up in Shinto shrines, except at the two important ones at Ise and Izumo. Today, Shinto shrines still exist alongside Buddhist temples in Nara, the ancient capital of Japan. However, after a thousand years a new patriotism developed, and with the Meiji restoration in 1867 the capital was moved to Tokyo and Shinto was cleansed of its Buddhist beliefs. Ryobu Shinto was abolished.

SELECT FOCUS | The mixing of religion with power politics, identifying faith with a flag, can cause great trouble, sometimes leading to war, as can be well documented in the history of Europe. Similarly in Japan, exposure to the modern world at the end of the nineteenth century created unease about foreign trading pressures and suspicions of Christian missionaries. Shinto as a result became increasingly seen as a tool for patriotism, providing nationalistic support for the government. It was viewed as a means for uniting the nation based upon traditional beliefs in the divine lineage of the emperor, who was able to trace his ancestry back to Amaterasu the sun goddess and who was therefore himself kami, divine. In 1946, at the end of the Second World War, this aspect of Shinto came, in retrospect, to be called State Shinto, so that it could be banned as a national ideology by the United States of America in the "Shinto Directive" while, at the same time, allowing the religious Shinto of the various sects to remain free.

SACRED TEXTS: *KOJIKI* AND *NIHONGI*
page 87
JAPANESE SHINTO
page 98
TENRI-KYO
page 102

TENRI-KYO

THE MAIN CONCEPT | Tenri-kyo (Religion of Heavenly Wisdom) was founded by an ordinary Japanese housewife, Nakayama Miki (1798–1887), originally a devotee of the Buddha Amida and his Pure Land. In 1838 she had a transforming religious experience, hearing what she took to be revelations and believing herself to be possessed by the "True God," the Lord of Heaven. Doubters questioned the genuine nature of her trances and she suffered some persecution, but she soon built up a following of people who listened to her oracles and who were convinced that she had powers of miraculous healing. Her cult, a mixture of Shinto with Buddhism, was finally recognized as one of the 13 Shinto sects in 1908; her divine mission was to save humankind, no less. Miki taught that human beings are fundamentally good but that this goodness is obscured by the "dust" of greed, which needs to be carefully wiped away. The "dust" leads to sickness, requiring faith-healing and purification. She greatly emphasized the importance of charitable deeds and the effectiveness of ecstatic dancing. The sect now has millions of followers; an enormous shrine in the new city of Tenri, near ancient Nara, marks the spot they take to be the center of creation, where one day "God the Parent" will descend to transform the world.

SELECT FOCUS | The existence of a great many sects within Shinto, of which 13 have been officially recognized by the Japanese government since the nineteenth century, is a good example of the natural tendency for religions to fragment over time. (There are also a dozen Buddhist sects in Japan.) Each Shinto sect has its own particular interest, such as teaching Confucian ethics against a Shinto background, or in worshipping the god of a particular mountain such as Fujiyama. Some with an emphasis on faith-healing may have been influenced by Christian ideas. Unlike earlier forms of Shinto practicing worship at local shrines, without any formal organization or systematized teaching, the Shinto sects, such as Tenri-kyo, were established by founders, formalized their beliefs, and produced religious texts. A marked feature of many of these new forms of Shinto is their practical emphasis, incorporating ethical and social ideals within a framework of faith. They flourish in modern Japan.

JAPANESE SHINTO
page 98
DUAL SHINTO
page 100

THE CULT
OF KWANNON

THE MAIN CONCEPT | The Japanese goddess of mercy, Kwannon (Kuan-yin in China), has perhaps the most extraordinary biography of all deities. She is a gentle "queen-of-heaven" figure, with many simple shrines erected to her, often by a lake, the sea, or a stream. Fishermen pray to her for protection when away from shore, as do pregnant women for a safe birth. Elegant statues in wood, plaster, or bronze portray her sitting at ease upon a rock by a spring of water. Devotees may practice meditation by repeating the mantra associated with her, "*Om-Mani-Padme-Hum*," quietly synchronizing its repetition with their breath. Some will have been trained by a guru to visualize her coming to them in a vision with a blessing. Strangely, devotion to this popular and compassionate figure began back in northern India as the veneration of a male Buddhist bodhisattva, Avalokiteśvara ("The One who surveys the world with compassion"). This saintly follower of Sakyamuni became, for a time, even more popular than the Buddha himself, with his own shrines and scriptures. His fame spread north into Nepal, Tibet, and Mongolia, where images of him bore a great resemblance to Tara, a Himalayan goddess. The two became confused and passed into China as Kuan-yin. The sex change was complete.

SELECT FOCUS | Part of the appeal of Mahayana Buddhism as it spread out of India was the development of devotion to divine beings who would share their hard-earned merit with their followers. They vowed to defer their entry into Nirvana out of compassion until all other sentient beings had been saved from the passions of desire, hate, and ignorance. Such a character was Avalokiteśvara; mere mention of his name brings salvation to a follower. He first appears in the 25th chapter of the great Mahayana scripture the Lotus Sutra, where he is praised for the benefits he confers on all his worshippers. He is an attendant to the Buddha Amida (or Amitabha) and is said to have many emanations, even appearing as Hindu gods, or Buddhas, in the interest of being able to teach the eternal truth to all creatures. It is even claimed that he created the world. Some statues portray these fantastic abilities by showing him symbolically with a thousand arms and many heads.

THERAVADA & MAHAYANA BUDDHISM
page 34

FALUN GONG

THE MAIN CONCEPT | A thread running through all of Chinese religion has been the physical, spiritual, and moral cultivation of the self, drawing in elements from Taoism, Confucianism, and Buddhism. Falun Gong, a new movement of self-improvement exhibiting these traits and attracting both secular and religious types of people, first erupted publicly in north-east China in the early 1990s with the teaching of Li Hongzhi. Li Hongzhi has lived in the USA since 1996. With its focus on disciplined slow-moving physical exercises, Falun Gong spread like wildfire and now has many tens of millions of practitioners both in China and worldwide. Alongside the emphasis on bodily health, the movement also teaches the need to cultivate virtue, guided by three tenets: truthfulness, compassion, and forbearance. By adopting these virtues practitioners believe that they identify with the fundamental nature of the universe, bringing their lives into harmony with what is good and true. The name Falun Gong, meaning literally "Dharma wheel practice," reveals its Buddhist origins, and its emblem combines the Taoist *yin-yang* symbol with the Indian swastika. But with no formal membership or hierarchical organization, the movement has an uneasy relationship with the authorities in China because of its great popularity and independent spirit.

SELECT FOCUS | One of the great gifts from China and Japan to the rest of the world has been the insistence that spiritual health also requires and depends on physical well-being; an inner awareness of the body is cultivated through disciplined daily exercises and mindful breathing. It has become a matter of normality, worldwide, to encounter groups in public places practicing the dignified movements of the martial art Tai chi (often in the early morning), each person turning with poise as though in slow-motion combat with an invisible adversary. Children in many countries attend classes in the more militant discipline of Taekwondo (promoting self-confidence, respect for others,

and self-defense), some progressing competitively to Olympic level. These disciplines, and many others, can, like Falun Gong, all be traced back to Buddhist, Taoist, and Confucian principles and to the linkage between meditation and physical self-control, body and mind working together in balanced harmony.

CONFUCIANISM
page 88

SOKA GAKKAI INTERNATIONAL

THE MAIN CONCEPT | One of the fastest-growing religions in the West today is a branch of Nichirenism from Japan, the Soka Gakkai International (Value Creation International), with its emphasis upon the need for human revolution whereby lay people take responsibility for their own growth. SGI was founded in 1975 as an international peace movement, on the island of Guam, close to the spot where bombers took off to deliver their nuclear devastation of Hiroshima and Nagasaki at the end of the Second World War. It has become a global network of affiliated organizations. Central to the religious practice of this movement is the twice-daily chanting, either privately or in groups, of the Sanskrit mantra "*nam-myoho-renge-kyo*"— "Hail to the Lotus of the True Law"—and of verses from the Lotus Sutra (see page 150) made popular in the thirteenth century by the Buddhist reformer Nichiren. The chanting is usually performed before a sacred scroll, the Gohonzon. The importance of study is also emphasized, alongside spiritual faith and chanting; to this end, discussion meetings are held monthly in the homes of followers, with topics ranging from the need for nuclear disarmament or same-sex marriage, to ways of combating racism in the community. Anyone can belong, whatever their cultural or religious background.

SELECT FOCUS | Mandalas have an important role in Buddhist worship, and perform for the eye visually what chanting a mantra does through sound. The famous psychologist Carl G. Jung wrote about the value of mandalas and the power they have for focusing and bringing together different parts of the mind. The original Gohonzon of Nichiren was inscribed by the founder in the thirteenth century; it is a scroll, a mandala, designed to aid devotion of the Lotus Sutra by opening a window, as it were, to Buddhahood. The title of the Lotus Sutra rises up through the heart of the Gohonzon in bold script, looking like a pagoda or the tower of a burial *stupa*, while around its corners are inscribed the names of gods and Buddhas who protect the teaching—those of the two great Buddhas, Sakyamuni and Prabhutaratna, being written across the top. Nichiren produced hundreds of versions of the Gohonzon; more modern variations are used in Soka Gakkai International.

BUDDHISM
page 32
BIOGRAPHIES: NICHIREN
page 85

THE BIRDMAN CULT OF EASTER ISLAND

THE MAIN CONCEPT | Few communities are as isolated as the inhabitants of the remote and tiny Polynesian island of Rapa Nui (Easter Island) in the South Pacific—their soccer players have no "away games," the next-nearest pitch being 2,300 miles (3,700 km) to the east. Yet even here the human urge to create religious ceremonies and rituals is evident. The dark rocks on the north side of the island display mysterious patterns and carvings cut deeply into the rough volcanic tuft; bird heads with powerful beaks are prominent (perhaps the frigate bird, that pirate of tropical seas) with crouching human bodies suggesting masked shamans. This is the Tangata manu Birdman cult, with its several deities, male and female, the chief one being the fertility god Make-make. Once a year, senior men on the island gathered for a dangerous competition: each appointed a young man to scramble down a precipitous cliff, swim a mile through shark-infested ocean to a remote rock, and there be the first to collect the egg of a migratory sooty tern. The sponsor of the winner was granted privileges for a year, shaved and painted his head, and was treated as sacred with religious power. The cult was banned by Christian missionaries in the 1860s.

SELECT FOCUS | Older than the Birdman cult are the immense and mysterious monolithic heads to be found all over Easter Island: called Moai, they have perplexed visitors ever since the island was "discovered" by Europeans in 1722. How were they carved? How were they moved? Why are they there? To stand at the foot of any of the over-eight hundred monumental heads is to experience being in the presence of something "other." Stylized in design, they stare peacefully out across the island (never out to sea), with an austere untroubled calm, as though keeping watch over the land. The era of their erection seems to have come to an abrupt end several hundred years ago, but some of the heads still lie on the flanks of a volcano at the south end of the island, resting like gods waiting to be born from the earth. It is generally thought that they represent ancestors and guardian spirits from a religious period about which we know nothing.

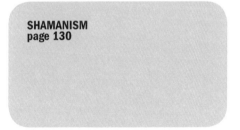

SHAMANISM
page 130

CARGO CULTS OF MELANESIA

THE MAIN CONCEPT | The disruption (mental, economic, and social) caused to isolated Melanesian communities in the Pacific Ocean by contact with the more technologically advanced nations of the world in the twentieth century led to the formation of a number of "cargo cults." "How come they have all this cargo?" was the question that unsettled the minds of many islanders as they encountered airplanes, vehicles, radios, canned food, and cola for the first time. Charismatic figures emerged in response to the social stress, often claiming to have had visions and promising a dramatic change in the social order. Their cults are often referred to, by anthropologists, as "millenarian," borrowing a concept from Christianity about the expected return of Christ and the ensuing millennium of peace. Apocalyptic beliefs held by some Christian missionaries may have contributed to the inflamed expectations of the cults. One of the most famous of these movements, developed after the Second World War on the island of Vanuatu, is the cult of John Frum—a legendary figure, sometimes visualized as a black American infantryman (the US Military were based there during the war), believed to live in the island's volcano. Someday, it is said, he will return with all the cargo dreamed of by his followers.

SELECT FOCUS | The response to charismatic figures (sometimes rather strange ones) among the cargo cults, exemplifies a human need that recurs throughout religious history, particularly in times of social stress. Is this feature a strength in our species or a weakness? Will we progress to a time when cult heroes are no longer needed? It is interesting to reflect that many of the great religions of today's world began as local cults; Jesus was a cult figure among Jews in Roman-occupied Judea; Mohammed gathered a small band of followers in Arabia; the Buddha built up a cult following of monks in northern India. What is it that makes one cult blossom into becoming a world religion

CHRISTIANITY
page 58
SPACE AGE CULTS
page 138

while another wilts on the stem? One intriguing cargo cult of Melanesia is that of the UK's Prince Philip, Duke of Edinburgh. At first, the Prince was unaware that he had been adopted as a deity by the Yaohnanen tribe on the southern island of Tanna in Vanuatu, their belief in his divinity being strengthened by a royal visit in 1974. He has since responded graciously to their attention.

I come to tell news;
I come to tell news.
The buffaloes are coming
again; The buffaloes are
coming again.
My father tells.
The Dead People are
coming again; The Dead
People are coming again.
My father tells.
The Earth will be made
new; the earth will be
made new.
Says the Mother.

GHOST DANCE SONG

4

AFRICA, AUSTRALIA & THE AMERICAS

I TRODUCTIO

The religions of Europe, Asia, and China have an ancient history; they've had time to evolve and divide into varying identifiable sects; to develop traditions with clear social structures and hierarchies; and above all to write and preserve collections of scriptures, venerated sacred texts, and to develop clearly formulated written creeds that encapsulate the fundamentals of their beliefs. When we look to Africa, Australia, and the Americas, we find a different state of affairs historically; tribal societies that have never needed to give an identifying name to their religions because they are simply what people do and believe. Religion is so much entwined with daily life that the two are virtually indistinguishable; traditions often have no remembered founders. These are communities that never developed writing and so have no literary tradition; stories and myths have been passed down orally from generation to generation. Nevertheless, these rich and colorful religious practices, each unique to its own community, have their own ancient ancestry. We rely on modern-day vocal witnesses from these peoples for what we know about them, and upon on the work of anthropologists and interested travelers.

The unconscious prejudice of European colonial rulers, such as in Africa, was to see all indigenous religions as "primitive," to label them as the superstitions of savages. Their ignorant assumptions about what constitutes "civilization" blinded them to the profound insights local tribes had into human nature and the relationship between people and the natural world around them; they rejected their local gods as unimportant, dismissing them as pagan, and for a long time ignored their religious art.

Veneration of the natural world

Tribal religion is often referred to as "animistic" (from Latin "'anima," meaning "soul" or "spirit") because of its treatment of the natural world as a spiritual reality, with trees, creatures, waterfalls, and mountains all having their own genius or soul. What surprised, or was overlooked by, many Christian missionaries was that while expressing reverence for a numberless multitude of spirits of nature, many primal (not primitive) faiths also believed in a Supreme Being—Wakan Tanka, the Great Spirit of many Native American tribes; or Chukwu (who has been described as "the immense overflowing source of all being") of the Nigerian Igbo tribe; or Olorun of the Yoruba. This confounded the nineteenth-century view that religion evolved from magic and superstition, through myth and polytheism, to the pinnacle of monotheism in Western European culture. The idea of there being one Supreme Being, a power beyond description, is not a new sophisticated development of faith—it was always there.

Much of tribal religion is expressed through dance in a sacred space inducing a state of trance. The dancers believe that they are able to control the evil spirits of illness (as traditionally performed, for example, by the False Face Society of the Iroquois, a woodland people of the north-west USA), or to summon ancestors (as in the Ghost Dance of the Sioux), or to renew the world (as in the four-day marathon of the Sun Dance by the Cheyenne). Dance, it is believed, generates spiritual power, which can be directed by the elders or a shaman. Painting, too, can generate magic power in many belief systems. Aboriginal artists in Australia using natural self-sourced earth colors believe they can re-enter the Dreamtime of myth and legend, and become part of spiritual history by being absorbed through imagination into the creative process. Among Native Americans there is the intriguing tradition of sandpainting, in which an elaborate picture in colored sands is created on the floor for the healing of the sick—and no sooner created but destroyed.

The impact of Western culture

Inevitably, the shock of expanding Western culture has taken its toll on these communities; some have been destroyed, like the Incas or the Aztecs, leaving only artefacts and impressive monuments. Foreign religions have swept across continents; missionary religions, Christian and Muslim throughout Africa; imported churches in Australia and New Zealand; Catholicism and varieties of Protestantism across the Americas; pockets of Hinduism, Buddhism, and Chinese ancestor worship everywhere. There have also been interesting innovations: Rastafarians, Mormons, and Pentecostalists. Pentecostalism, a Christian Protestant religion, is currently on the ascendency throughout South America, attracting young families in their hundreds of thousands to its exuberant worship and presenting a challenge to the traditional Catholic churches of the region. The Mormons have a very recent history, dating from 1830 in New York State. They combine an intriguing appeal to ancient legends about some Israelites arriving in America two and a half thousand years ago, with a Protestant Puritan view of life and their own dream of a Promised Land. Very different in lifestyle are the Rastafarians in Jamaica, who also trace their ancestry back to the Israelites, but in their case via Ethiopia.

BIOGRAPHIES

MARCUS GARVEY (1887–1940)

Marcus Garvey was considered to be a prophet by the Rastafarian community because he predicted the appearance of a Black Messiah in Africa, whose coming would herald a new era in world history, with Africa at its heart. He foresaw in his vision and dream of the future that Africans who were dispersed around the world, many as the result of slavery organized by European colonial powers, would return from this *diaspora* to their true homeland. The crowning of Emperor Haile Selassie in Ethiopia in 1933 seemed to fulfill this prediction—it was certainly seen as so by Rastafarians. Born in Jamaica, Garvey was raised as a Methodist (though later he became a Roman Catholic); he traveled as a young man through the Caribbean and Central America, working and writing, and then spent two years in the UK in London, where he studied at Birkbeck College. Returning to Jamaica he began to do something about his belief that Africans should enjoy civil rights and economic freedom by organizing the Universal Negro Improvement Association. In 1916 he moved to the USA where, as an editor and publisher, he became famous as a black activist with a powerful religious and political vision. His energy led him into various business ventures, some of which were successful (though not the Black Star Shipping Line, which went bankrupt), and he even attempted to organize a new homeland for black Americans in Liberia, North Africa. He inevitably met with opposition and spent a short time in jail accused of fraud. He died in London, but his body was later moved to Jamaica; Martin Luther King visited his shrine there in 1965 and, praising him in a speech, said that: "He was the first man on a mass scale and level to give millions of Negroes a sense of dignity and destiny."

BLACK ELK (1863–1950)

Black Elk lived primarily in South Dakota, USA. He formed an invaluable bridge between Western Christian culture and the religion and spirituality of the Oglala Lakota, a branch of the Sioux, traveling to Europe in his youth with Buffalo Bill's Wild West Troupe and later in life becoming Nicholas Black Elk, a baptized Roman Catholic. He was a medicine man, experiencing visions from the age of nine and throughout his life. His initial vision is described in detail in what was to become a cult book in the 1960s, *Black Elk Speaks*, based on interviews by John Neihardt. In this vision he hears voices calling him and is taken into the sky, which is filled with dancing horses and flocks of geese, and in which he rides in the storm clouds: six grandfathers speak to him and he realizes that they are the powers from all six directions in the world—north, south, east, west, up, and down. He is given sacred herbs, a peace pipe and a magic bright red stick, which, on flying down from the sky as a spotted eagle, he plants at the center of a village and instantly it grows into a giant cottonwood tree full of birds and sheltering all types of animals mingling with the people. He sees suffering and starvation across the world and yet feels compelled to sing a song with the words "A good nation I will make live." He subsequently felt that he had a mission in life to rebuild the fortunes of his tribe, re-establishing, for example, the Lakota version of the Sun Dance while working as a medicine man and a healer.

ROVER THOMAS (1926–98)

Rover Thomas is one of the best-known aboriginal artists, whose energy and inspiration comes from the Dreamtime. His parents came from the Kujaka and the Wangkajunga people, and he was born by Well 33 on the Canning Stock Route, bordering the Great Sandy Desert. From the age of ten he worked as a stockman across the Northern Territories, but he returned home to the East Kimberley region while still a young man, where he became an artist in Turkey Creek. His first paintings were on boards used in the aboriginal narrative dance cycle of a ceremony called the Kurirr. The themes came to him from the Dreaming (source of all true knowledge), he claimed; nothing was invented by him. The use of earth pigments in a unique style, with powerful simple imagery, makes his work instantly recognizable. The cycle tells of the journey made by the spirit of an old lady returning home to Turkey Creek from Perth, where she had died following a road accident caused by a cyclone and a swollen creek. Meandering over the landscape, she sees the sites of historical massacres, and encounters Dreamtime beings and the mythical Rainbow Serpent.

SACRED TEXTS

THE FLORENTINE CODEX

Much of what we know about Aztec religion comes from an amazing document called the Florentine Codex, composed in the sixteenth century, then lost, only to re-emerge in the eighteenth century in a library in Florence, Italy—hence its name. The author was a remarkable man, Bernardino de Sahagún (1499–1590), a Franciscan friar credited to be the world's first anthropologist (see page 129). It may be that its two-hundred-year "disappearance" had something to do with the suspicions of the Spanish Inquisition, which would not have taken kindly to a sympathetic investigation into a non-Catholic religion. The copy in Florence came into the hands of the Medici family in the late sixteenth century. The original Spanish work in four volumes was entitled *Historia general de las cosas de la Nueva Espana* (General History of the Things of New Spain). De Sahagún's missionary motive in writing was to understand the customs and religion of the conquered people in order to make it easier to convert them to Christianity;

inevitably he was repelled by some of the things he discovered, such as human sacrifice, though he admired other elements of Aztec sophistication and culture. He conducted his ethnographic research with the help of local Nahuatl-speaking people, recording their words phonetically and providing a Spanish translation. The work is illustrated by over two thousand pictures created by local artists. The 12 books of the codex begin with a description of the Aztec gods, followed by a detailed account of their religious ceremonies including the horrifying sacrifice of a 13-year-old girl dressed up to be the maize goddess Chicomecohuatl (described on page 129). The final book contains a description, from the point of view of the conquered, of Hernán Cortés, the Spanish conquistador whose expedition in the sixteenth century brought about the fall of the Aztec Empire.

THE FIRST BOOK OF KINGS

The relationship between the famous King Solomon of Jerusalem and the Queen of Sheba three thousand years ago has become the subject of legend. The earliest accounts of this romantic encounter are to be found in the First Book of Kings (sixth century BCE) in an historical section of the Bible comprising two Books of Samuel and two of Kings. The story that blossomed from this text was that the Queen of Sheba married King Solomon and, returning to Ethiopia in Africa, took with her a large entourage of Israelites (see page 140). Although there is no mention in the Bible of a marriage between the two, the Jews of Ethiopia have drawn on this tale to authenticate their religion. In the twentieth century Rastafarians referred to the same legend to establish their belief that they too were God's chosen people. The biblical texts finally edited in the sixth century BCE, when the Jews were exiled in Babylon, draw on earlier documents no longer available to historians; a History of Solomon, the Annals of the Kings of Israel, and the Annals of the Kings of Judah. King Solomon was famous in his day both for his wealth and for his wisdom. It was he who built the magnificent Temple in Jerusalem that became the earthly focus of the Jewish religion. But Solomon was not without his faults, and some were to have severe consequences for Israel: he had 700 wives (many were probably foreign marriages contracted for political ends) and many concubines. He allowed his foreign wives to import their own gods and to build shrines to them; a practice denounced by those faithful to the God of Abraham, Isaac, and Jacob as the great sin, banned in the Ten Commandments, of "bowing the knee to Baal." Such religious laxity was later seen as the cause of the break-up of Israel into two kingdoms after Solomon's death and their subsequent conquest by foreign nations.

SANDPAINTINGS OF THE NAVAJO SHOOTING CHANT

Sandpaintings, created in very private ceremonies where cameras are forbidden and alien observers rare, are designed to be destroyed in the same day they are produced. This presents a problem for the anthropologist of religious practice. Fortunately, research by two dedicated women has brought an appreciation of the sandpainting of the Navajo (see page 132) to a wider audience. Gladys A. Reichard and Franc J. Newcomb published in 1937 their detailed observations in the *Sandpaintings of the Navajo Shooting Chant*. Reichard spent five summers living with the family of the singer of a Shooting Chant, and was allowed to sit in and observe the singing and creation of pictures in sand of this healing ceremony. She even had a Chant sung over her to "make it safe" for her to handle the sensitive material she garnered. Franc Newcomb, meanwhile, had, with the permission of the Chanters, found a way to record the ephemeral art form. She watched carefully, memorizing every detail as the painting was created; then, leaving the Hogan, she made her own copy in watercolors. On checking these later, the chanters were delighted to see how good her recordings were.

YORUBA RELIGION

THE MAIN CONCEPT | The Yoruba, a group of people numbered in millions, occupy western parts of Nigeria; their major center, the city of Ife, was founded almost a thousand years ago. Many, through the slave trade, finished up living in the New World, taking with them their cultural and religious practices, some of which are still honored. Belief in religious power is fundamental to Yoruba religion. All power comes from Olorun (literally "Owner of the Sky"), the High God, who generated all the power of the cosmos; he is a remote figure with no shrines or direct contact with the Yoruba. Power comes from him to the world via lesser deities—the Orisa—of whom there are hundreds associated with local clans, sacred places, and aspects of nature. Priesthoods and diviners, mediums and masked dancers, serve the Orisa, providing access for the people. Beneath the Orisa are the ancestors; they also wield power and are approached by the head of each family through rituals at the family shrine. Some Orisa were once ancestors; the popular god of metal, Ogun, is said to have been a king—Nigerian truck drivers often carry a representation of him, because of his association with metal: a charm to protect them from accidents. Sorcerers and witches (respectable roles in Yoruba society) draw their power from the earth.

MARA THE EVIL ONE
page 36
CHINESE ANCESTOR WORSHIP
page 96

SELECT FOCUS | It is a universal experience that things can go wrong in life. Religions accommodate this uncomfortable fact through stories of a trickster or troublemaker, tempter or joker. Teutonic myth had its Loki, Native Americans their Coyote: Satan, Mara, trolls, and goblins—the list of forces that create havoc in life is a long one. For the Yoruba the mischief-maker is Esu. His role is complex for he is an intermediary between Olorun and human beings, but also contains good and evil in his character. An extension of Olorun's power, he provides tests—such as introducing accidents into life—to determine and strengthen people's characters. He has no shrines of his own but is present at every shrine when offerings and prayers are being made, and must be acknowledged. He may nudge the priest or head of a family into making a mistake that gives offense to some deity, thus bringing trouble in its wake. His watchful eye and invisible presence ensures that worshippers are vigilant.

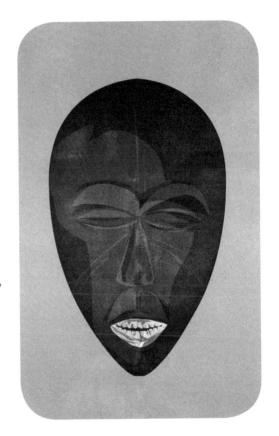

ABORIGINAL DREAMTIME

THE MAIN CONCEPT | The Dreamtime is not just "Once upon a time," it is *now*; not just a time in the past, but an ever-present reality. In the Australian aboriginal belief system the world was sung into existence by the totemic ancestors who created the Australian landscape as they walked across the original barren surface of the world. Singing, they brought every rock, bluff, waterhole, and desert oak; every patch of mallee scrubland and spinifex grass; into existence. Their tracks created the Songlines that are sung today and through which the aborigine, by re-entering the Dreaming, identifies with his or her land and ancestors; they are inseparable. The Dreamtime stories, emerging from 40,000 years of aboriginal culture, contain knowledge about herbs, tribal law, and proper behavior; they identify certain places as being sacred, such as Uluru, the great sandstone monolith in the Red Centre; or it may be a range of mountains locally identified as the body of an ancestral snake. Every tribe has its own name for this creative spirituality, from which the storyteller and the artist draw their inspiration, power, and imagery. It was anthropologists in the nineteenth century who coined the term Dreamtime, trying to capture the essence of an immersive belief system that is both "then" and "now."

SELECT FOCUS | It is not hard to imagine why Uluru, the great sandstone rock in Australia's Northern Territory, should be treated as a sacred site by the local Anangu Pitjantjatjara aboriginal people. Nineteenth-century European explorers named it Ayers Rock, but it has since reverted to its original name. Molded by baking sun and rain over eons, it looks ancient (it is in fact almost 600 million years old); dry water gullies run down its sides, waterholes surround the base, rock shelters provide shade, its massive mysterious presence dominates the bush. It is a complex religious site: entering its various fissures and caves, associated with gender-related initiation ceremonies, is taboo, and photography is forbidden. One of the walking routes that are associated with the creation of this landscape through song passes by the rock, and Dreamtime tales tell of struggles between ancestral snakes in the creation of the monolith. Indeed, one rock pool here is consecrated to the "all knowing and everlasting" serpent. Climbing the sacred rock has been reluctantly permitted, but will be banned from 2019.

BIOGRAPHIES: ROVER THOMAS
page 119

MĀORI RELIGION

THE MAIN CONCEPT | An important concept found in Māori religion is *tapu*, meaning "sacred" or "holy," with the added implication of being untouchable, even dangerous. It is related to the Eastern Polynesian word *tabu*, which James Cook brought back to England at the end of the eighteenth century, from which we get the useful word "taboo," used to describe a society's rejection of certain types of behavior or to indicate topics to be avoided in discussion. The Māoris, exploring the Pacific Ocean from Eastern Polynesia, arrived in New Zealand in the thirteenth century, bringing with them veneration of their ancestors and belief in many deities, as well as the strong sense that some things are *tapu*. Iconic in the culture are the powerfully expressive carved faces of gods and ancestors; it is believed that gods communicate with people via the skill of a master craftsman. Shavings from such carvings are consequently *tapu*. Similar expressions are seen on the faces of the All Blacks rugby team when they perform their *haka*, their grimaces and foot stamping providing a graphic demonstration of power before a match. Māori mythology is colorful and complex, tracing the world's creation through alternating periods of darkness and light, and generations of gods culminating in Rangi and Papa, Father Sky and Mother Earth, from whom all Māoris are said to be descended.

CHINESE ANCESTOR WORSHIP
page 96

SELECT FOCUS | A typical example of a Māori myth is the tale of Maui (a culture hero and trickster with the ability to be transformed into a bird). Maui desperately wants to go fishing with his elder brothers. The brothers fob him off with excuses until, one day, he hides himself in their boat and sets out to sea. At first they are annoyed and believe that he will bring them bad luck, but after he recites an old magic incantation they haul in a great quantity of fish. When his turn comes to fish, the brothers will not share their bait, so he uses his own blood, drawn from his nose, to bait the pre-prepared hook. The fish he drags up from the deep is so enormous that it becomes the island Te Ika-a-Maui (the Fish of Maui), the North Island of New Zealand. A valuable collection of such myths, containing this tale and others, has been put together for schools by the New Zealand Ministry of Education.

AZTECS

THE MAIN CONCEPT | The civilization of the Aztecs (the "Crane People") spanned almost three centuries, from roughly 1248, when they arrived as nomadic people from the north, until 1521, when the Spanish conquistador Hernán Cortés conquered the empire, destroying its elaborate and cruel religious system. The gods of Aztec religion are too many to name or number; the Aztecs brought their own deities with them, and adopted those of neighboring tribes and of earlier Central American cultures, establishing control over other societies through force and a powerful priesthood. The temples they built (particularly the great pyramid at Tenochtitlan), many of which survive today, with their great plazas for religious rituals, bear impressive witness to all they were able to achieve. Human sacrifice permeated the religion—it is claimed that over 10,000 captives were sacrificed as a dedication to the gods when the temple at Tenochtitlan was erected. Shrines to the most important gods sit at the top of this and other pyramids: to the rain god Tlaloc and the sun god Huitzilopochtli ("Hummingbird Wizard"); to Quetzalcoatl ("Feathered Serpent") and his enemy Tezcatlipoca ("Smoking Mirror"). In religious mythology worldwide, the gods are often said to be self-sacrificing, representing the death and rebirth of the seasons. The Aztec priesthood, in a perversion of these stories, acted them out with human sacrifice.

SELECT FOCUS | Maize was an important crop for the Aztecs and was represented by its own goddess Chicomecohuatl. In myth she died and rose again each year. A festival in September re-enacts her sacrifice in the belief that this action will magically control nature. We have a detailed sixteenth-century account of one such by a Franciscan friar, Fray Bernardino Sahagún (see page 120). People prepared for the ceremony with a seven-day fast. They then chose a thirteen-year-old slave girl, dressed her up as the maize goddess Chicomecohuatl, and led her in a processional dance from house to house. Celebrations continued all night.

The following day she was carried to the temple of the sun god Huitzilopochtli to show her respects to the deity. Then all the elders, followed by all the women, bowed low, worshipping the girl as the embodiment of the goddess. The next morning, after incensing her and laying her down on a sheaf of corn, they cut off her head, and a priest wearing her bloody skin danced around the town.

SACRED TEXTS: THE FLORENTINE CODEX
page 120

SHAMANISM

THE MAIN CONCEPT | Shamanism is not in itself a religion, but has been described as an "archaic technique of ecstasy" to be found in many religious cultures around the world, through Africa, Asia, the Americas, and elsewhere. Evidence of the phenomenon can also be found in ancient mythology such as in the Greek story of Orpheus making a journey to the underworld; or in tales of Odin, in Norse mythology, taking to the air in mystical flight on his eight-legged horse Sleipnir. The word *shaman* comes from a Siberian language, Tungusic. The shaman breaks the normal bounds of human experience by practicing ecstasy, either through some personal psychic abnormality, or by the use of drugs, dance, or drumming; he or she is then able to "leave the body" to explore the cosmos, ascend into heaven, or plunge into the underworld, to return with information not available to more earthbound people, or to reunite the lost souls of the sick with their bodies. In Siberia the shaman reputedly rides for these journeys on the spirit of a sacrificed horse. The Inuit of the Arctic believe their shamans are able in their trance-like state to locate seals and even shepherd them to shore; while Sioux shamans claimed they could "see" herds of buffalo beyond the horizon.

SELECT FOCUS | The North American Orpheus myth is the name given to a "shamanic"-type tale with many common features to be found in a wide variety of Native American communities. They all have to do with attempts to bring back a loved one, such as a wife or sister from the dead, involving a dangerous journey to the next world, which lies somewhere in the West. The fearful inevitability of death has generated all of these stories. In the version of a tribe called the Telumni Yokuts, a man follows his wife after her death on a mystical journey until he comes to an unstable bridge across a stream, guarded by a bird, and she warns him not to follow. Protected by a magic talisman, he crosses to the land of the dead, where he is warmly welcomed and told that he can take his wife home after a night with her if he succeeds in a task: not to fall asleep. Inevitably he fails and returns to his friends alone.

INUIT RELIGION
page 134

THE NAVAJO

THE MAIN CONCEPT | The Navajo, Native Americans of the southwestern USA known as the Dine, have a strong belief in the importance of their relationship with the land around them, to the Earth Mother and the Sky Father, and to the four sacred mountains that define their territory: Blanca Peak and Hesperus Mountain in Colorado; Mount Taylor in New Mexico, and San Francisco Peaks in Arizona. It is a fundamental belief of their religion that they should live in harmony with the natural world. The purpose of all ceremonial dance, song, and chant is to establish and keep a proper balance in nature and in the health of individual members of the tribe, to prevent and cure diseases, or to protect from evil. Their elaborate myths tell how their distant ancestors emerged from Mother Earth and traveled through three worlds, each of which was destroyed, one involving a great flood. Finally they settled in their own territory, the present fourth world (the number four is sacred in ritual and storytelling). They refer to themselves as the Earth People and are helped or hindered in their lives by supernatural beings known as the Holy People. As with their relationship to Nature they strive to live in harmony with these powerful beings. In this the Navajo appeal to and are helped by the Holy People, their gods.

**SACRED TEXTS: *SANDPAINTINGS OF THE NAVAJO SHOOTING CHANT*
page 121**

SELECT FOCUS | It is a distinctive peculiarity of religious sandpaintings that they are created to be destroyed. They generate magic power that can be directed to the healing of a patient; but the power has to be released from the painting by destruction: it is temporary and, like all things in this world, ephemeral. The production of transitory pictures, mostly on the ground, using different-colored sands and natural pigments can be found in many traditions: those produced by the Navajo are among the finest. A much-respected member of the tribe is the Chanter. It is he who is responsible for choosing and organizing a Chant, which may last from one to nine days. He also selects the myth to be sung and the painter who will gather the materials for the painting. The whole performance takes place in a Hogan, the traditional dwelling of the Navajo. The symbolic and stylized pictures may be of rattles and snakes, trumpets and arrows, corn bugs and pollen, yellow or black wind, or thunder of various colors. Holy people, gods, and sky people are regular images.

INUIT RELIGION

THE MAIN CONCEPT | The religion of the Inuit in the Arctic has been molded by their harsh environment; freezing temperature and darkness, snow storm and shifting ice flow, threatening sea and roaming polar bear: and always, whatever the conditions, the need for food to survive. As with all primal religions, there are no organized hierarchies of power, no central authority to coordinate beliefs; a large body of mythology helps to interpret life, while respect for the many spirits of nature predominates. Inuit believe that the world is controlled by a multitude of invisible forces or "Innua." Everything in Nature has its own Innua—the sea, the sky, animals, even rocks—which may be helpful and become guardian familiar spirits; the Innua of stones and bears are especially powerful. If the Innua of a bear becomes a man's familiar, he may become an Angakok (a shaman or sorcerer) with the power to make good or bad weather, to locate the whereabouts of seals, to discover crimes through second sight, and so forth. Fear of those elements of Nature that seem malevolent is fuel for religion, calling for the services of the Angakok. Most feared, understandably, by the Inuit is the unpredictable sea goddess Sedna, said to be hostile to the human race.

SELECT FOCUS | The story of Sedna is well known in Inuit circles, and has many variations. She is sometimes described as being monstrously large, with one eye and fingerless hands. Said to have been the beautiful and much adored daughter of a fisherman, she spurned all suitors until one day a handsome man arrived in a boat and offered her all sorts of wealth to attract her attention. Reluctantly, she responded to his advances and went with him, leaving her distraught father. Her hopes turned sour when she discovered her lover to be a phantom created by a bird spirit—typically, in the legend, a fulmar petrel or a loon. Her father pursued and found her, but

SHAMANISM
page 130

when he set off with her for home the angry spirit stirred up such a storm that the father became terrified and threw Sedna overboard to pacify the waves. She clung desperately to the boat, upon which he chopped off her fingers, which became seals, walruses, and whales; Sedna sank into the deep, where she rules as a much-feared sea goddess.

THE GHOST DANCE

THE MAIN CONCEPT | It is a major function of religion to provide a group with social cohesion, and dancing together strengthens a sense of belonging, as well as generates hope and healing. Religious dance unites the dancers in a common dream, and there can be no better example than the Ghost Dance performed by Native American tribes west of the Mississippi. It began in 1889 when a Paiute medicine man named Wovoka (influenced perhaps by a solar eclipse that year and Christian speculation current at the time concerning the End of Days) had a dream that the Great Spirit was to send a devastating flood. He would roll up the old world like a carpet and create a new world for the Native American tribes. Gone would be the white man's iron snake and whispering wire (railroad and telegraph); his fences and his guns—the buffalo would once more roam the plains and the dead would return to their beautiful land. The non-violent but exhausting Ghost Dance, performed by the Arapaho, Cheyenne, Sioux, and others, helped the dancers share his dream; they danced in a circle holding hands, with no music, only voices; some collapsed from fatigue. White settlers and government agents were suspicious; the movement was suppressed with guns at the Massacre of Wounded Knee. Some still do the dance today.

SELECT FOCUS | Fatigue and exhaustion were taken a stage further involving the self-infliction of extreme pain in one of the most famous of the American Indian dances, the Sun Dance (revived by Black Elk for the Lakota people in the twentieth century—see page 119), performed on the Great Plains in summer for the healing of individuals, and for the renewal of the world. The Cheyenne called it the "New Life Lodge" ceremony and it illustrates a theme found in many tribal religions: the awareness of humanity's dependence on Nature and the need to live in rhythm with natural processes. The Sun Dance is a grueling challenge for the dancers, lasting four days with fasting from food and water, and for some it involves the torturous addition of hooks fastened into the body skin and linked by thongs to a central pole. The central pole represents the center of the world; a fork at the top provides space for a nest of the Thunder Bird, the Spirit who controls the sun and the rain. The dance is performed to the beat of drums and the shrill sound of eagle-bone whistles in a sacred circle marked out by stakes. For many years the dance was banned by the government: it's now been revived, but non-indigenous people are discouraged from attending.

BIOGRAPHIES: BLACK ELK
page 119

SPACE AGE CULTS

THE MAIN CONCEPT | With the turn of the millennium and astrological claims that we are entering the Age of Aquarius, and with traditional religions being questioned by a generation steeped in science and technology, there has been a blossoming of hundreds of New Age cults all over the globe. Most of them, typically led by a cult figure, draw on older religions for their beliefs—on Buddhism, the Vedanta, Hinduism, or Christianity, for example. A small minority are accused of brainwashing and controlling their vulnerable followers, but the majority are benign, offering companionship and a moral worldview full of hope. Among these, some of the most intriguing are the Space Age Cults. They look to the skies for salvation, excited by the thought that there are aliens "out there" with greater wisdom and technological skill than humanity; their gods have been described as "angels in space suits." The appeal depends in part on an age-old belief in sky gods. The Aetherius Society, founded in the UK in the 1950s by George King, was officially incorporated in the USA in 1960, with its HQ in Los Angeles. It now claims to be a worldwide organization, believing in the existence of superior extra-terrestrial intelligences whom its members call The Cosmic Masters, and in an Interplanetary Parliament.

SELECT FOCUS | The group known as The Heaven's Gate Cult hit the front pages of the world press when all 39 members committed suicide together in a neatly orchestrated event. Founded in San Diego, California, in 1974 by Marshall Applewhite and Bonnie Nettles, the cult came to its tragic end in 1997. The two founders both came from Christian backgrounds with a strong belief in biblical prophecy, and were convinced that they were the "two witnesses" referred to in the Book of Revelation; superior beings with a special mission on earth. Applewhite was also an avid reader of science fiction. The well-educated disciples believed themselves to be living on the edge of a new era in evolution in which they would no longer need their physical bodies but would rise to "The Evolutionary Level above Human." Upon their suicide they expected their spirits to be transported to join the crew of a massive futuristic spaceship flying in the wake of the comet Hale-Bopp on its appearance in 1997.

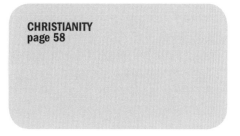

CHRISTIANITY
page 58

RASTAFARIANISM

THE MAIN CONCEPT | Rastafarians take their name
from Ras Tafari (1892–1975), Prince Tafari of Ethiopia,
who became Emperor Haile Selassie, believed by them
(though not by him) to be the Messiah Jesus Christ, or God
(whom they call Jah—the biblical Jehovah). His appearance
on earth had been predicted by the popular black activist
Marcus Garvey and heralded a proud new era for Black
Africa. Rastafarian religion gets strength and meaning
from tapping into ancient stories and legends associated
with the Israelites and the Old Testament. The Ethiopian
Queen of Sheba visited, and many believe became the
wife of, King Solomon in Jerusalem; she returned home
accompanied, according to legend, by a large cohort of
Israelites (see page 120). Haile Selassie claimed to be the
225th descendant from this romantic affair, one of his
many titles being "Lion of the Tribe of Judah." Rastafarians
in Jamaica, whose ancestors were slaves from Africa, see
themselves (with only a vague sense of geography) as
inheritors of the Israelites in the Ethiopian story. Picking
up on another theme from Israelite history, they claim to
be God's chosen people and see Africa as their Promised
Land, to which they will return. They are a proudly
recognizable community, hair in dreadlocks, wearing
traditional colors—red, black, and green—and smoking
ganja (marijuana) in their prayer meetings.

PROPHETS
page 56

BIOGRAPHIES: MARCUS GARVEY
page 118

SACRED TEXTS: THE FIRST BOOK
OF KINGS
page 120

SELECT FOCUS | The reggae music of the Jamaican songwriter and performer Bob Marley (1945–81) has been enjoyed by millions internationally; particularly important are the words that emanate from his Rastafarian beliefs. He smoked marijuana (and was arrested for it in London), strongly believing it to be a God-given herb, a sacrament with spiritual value, evidence for which he found in references to "grass" (another of its names) in the Bible (for example, Psalm 104:14). With the Wailers, Marley released some of his earliest reggae records; after they were disbanded, in 1974, Marley went on to release records on his own, one of the most famous being the album *Exodus*. "Exodus" is a biblical word full of resonance, recalling God leading his people out of slavery in Egypt to their own Promised Land. Other songs on the album refer to Babylon, where the Jews were exiled in the fifth century BCE. For Marley, Babylon represented the white Western world, with its white portrayals of Jesus; but God, he believed, had now revealed himself in Africa, and he was black.

MORMONS

THE MAIN CONCEPT | Virtually all religions build upon earlier foundations, and in the modern era Mormonism (otherwise known as The Church of Jesus Christ of Latter-Day Saints) in the USA is a good example. Founded in 1830 by Vermont-born Joseph Smith II (1805–44), who had visions of angels, it established itself within a generation in Salt Lake City, Utah, as a respectable new/old American religion with legendary links to the Children of Israel and Jesus Christ. Smith was guided, he believed, by an angel Moroni to a spot in New York State to find The Book of Mormon written on golden tablets in an unknown language (Reformed Egyptian), which he was able to translate with the aid of some magical objects called Urim and Thummim (mysterious religious objects featured in the Hebrew Bible). The book offered a link to the last of a lost tribe of Israelites who had supposedly been wiped out by Native Americans in the fifth century CE, having emigrated there a thousand years earlier. Jesus Christ was said to have visited these people after his ascension. The new movement of Latter-Day Saints quickly attracted followers and settled in Ohio, then later in Illinois; they attracted opposition, particularly over Smith's policy of allowing polygamy. The great event that solidified the religion was the heroic trek to Utah (see opposite).

JUDAISM
page 54

PROPHETS
page 56

CHRISTIANITY
page 58

SELECT FOCUS | An epic journey that has become part of legend, firmly established the Mormons in American history. Joseph Smith had been assassinated when in jail and the leadership of the Latter-Day Saints passed to Brigham Young (1801–77). The tight-knit and now prosperous community experienced hostility and violence from neighbors. Fifteen thousand men, women, and children, with thousands of cattle, left Illinois and headed west into the wilderness in 1846. For them this momentous trek had biblical echoes of the sufferings of the Israelites in Egypt; this was their Exodus in search of their own Promised Land. Arriving in Utah, then Mexican territory, the community toiled hard, often against the odds, and established Salt Lake City as their headquarters. Their life was disciplined and frugal, with puritanical values that were a great attraction to

some, including abstention from alcohol, coffee, and tea. Missionaries were sent out to make new converts. The building of railroads across America put an end to their seclusion, and when Utah finally became part of the United States, Mormons had to renounce polygamy.

PE TECOSTALISTS

THE MAIN CONCEPT | Pentecostalism, which is now sweeping Latin America, challenging Catholicism as the principal Christian church in the region, has its roots in European Protestantism, although it only became a recognizable revival movement early in the twentieth century. Globally it has almost 300 million followers. It takes its name from the so-called Day of Pentecost recorded in the New Testament Book of Acts, when, in around 33 CE, Jewish disciples of the crucified Jesus Christ gathered together in an upper room fearful for their lives, only to be unexpectedly overcome by what they understood to be a powerful experience of the Holy Spirit. Pentecostalism's emphasis in life and worship, therefore, is on a direct personal experience of God through the gift of the Spirit, which is seen as the mark of the true believer and is referred to as being baptized in the Spirit. Services, which are described as being charismatic, arouse religious enthusiasm and ecstasy in worshippers, and often include the phenomenon of speaking in tongues. The emotional liberation that comes from being able to "let go" in the safe company of like-minded people is extremely attractive to some believers and is not an experience they find in more traditional liturgies. The Pentecostal movement is infectious and is inspiring some congregations in other Christian denominations.

SELECT FOCUS | Speaking in tongues (technically called *glossolalia*—a Greek term) is a phenomenon experienced by some worshippers when in a trance-like state; they lose all inhibition and speak either in a different language or in some unrecognizable tongue. The phenomenon occurs in many religions, but in Christianity it is seen as the fulfillment of a promise made by God through the Old Testament prophet Joel, anticipating a new messianic era: "I shall pour out my Spirit on all humanity. Your sons and daughters shall prophesy . . . " Members of the early Christian church and Pentecostalists interpreted this to mean speaking in tongues, as they experienced at Pentecost. The event is described in the Book of Acts, the Holy Spirit coming to them from the sky like a rushing mighty wind followed by flames of fire settling on each of their heads. They spoke in tongues and a large crowd of foreigners were astonished to understand what they said "in their own language."

CHRISTIANITY
page 58
PROTESTANTISM
page 62

RELIGIONS & ECOLOGY

THE MAIN CONCEPT | The task facing religions as they seek to embrace ecology is challenging. Conservative prejudices will have to be overturned, and searches made to locate within their traditions any seeds of insight that could become the foundations of a new way of looking at our place and responsibility in Nature. Religions that believe in Mother Earth, sometimes called Gaia, and animistic religions believing in the spirits of nature, have much to offer as humanity struggles to get away from the arrogant idea that the natural world is there for us to plunder. Christians and Jews will have to go back to their Bibles to reassess the relationship between people and the ecosystem, turning away, perhaps, from the Genesis creation stories in which man is given dominion over creation, and focusing instead on passages like Psalm 104, in which the psalmist paints a rich picture of the natural world in which the human being going out to work is just one small element in the scene. Many colleges in the USA and elsewhere now offer courses in the new and important discipline of Religion and Ecology. The future of all—fish, wild animals, insects, trees, and people—depends on what we choose to do.

SELECT FOCUS | A spirituality that does not recognize that human beings are products of nature and of the chemistry of the earth is missing something fundamentally important. All living creatures are fellow mortals; we all share in the same interconnected web of life that covers the planet. In fact the earth itself, wrapped in its relatively thin layer of living matter, the biosphere, can be seen as a single self-regulating organism. It was this insight that led James Lovelock in 1979 to formulate the Gaia Hypothesis. The goddess Gaia—Mother Earth—in Greek mythology was a personification of the earth who, with Uranus, parented all the Olympian gods. Purists among the monotheistic religions may feel uneasy about personalizing nature as Mother Earth in this way, but it is done in the same spirit as that of the thirteenth-century St. Francis of Assisi in his *Canticle of the Sun*. He praises God for, and through, his creations of Brother Sun and Sister Moon, Brother Wind and Sister Water, Brother Fire and Sister Mother Earth.

JUDAISM
page 54
CHRISTIANITY
page 58

GLOSSARY

ADVAITA—A spiritual doctrine developed by the Vedanta school of Indian philosophy, meaning that there is no distinction between the individual person and Brahman (ultimate reality). Literally, they are "not two."

AHIMSA—Non-violence; the peaceful response to all of life's challenges taught by the Jain religion. It involves respect for all living creatures.

AMITABHA—The principal Buddha, seen as a savior, in Pure Land Buddhism, a branch of the Mahayana tradition.

ANATTA—Literally "no soul" or "no self." The difficult teaching in Buddhism that the concept of each of us having a separate soul or being a separate individual is an illusion and part of the cause of suffering.

ANIMISM—(From the Latin for "breath" or "spirit.") The belief found worldwide in earliest forms of religion that the natural world is inhabited by spirits; that all of nature, whether rocks, trees, mountains, or rivers, has its own living spiritual essence. The belief survives in many contemporary religions such as Shinto and Hinduism.

ARHATS—A respected person within Buddhism who has gained insight into the true nature of reality and is well on the path to complete Enlightenment.

ATMAN—The name given to the self or soul in Indian spirituality.

AVATAR—A Sanskrit term, meaning "descent," this refers to the incarnation and physical appearance of a deity on earth. There are said to have been ten avatars of the god Vishnu, for example, the most famous being Krishna, the leading character in the *Bhagavad Gita*.

AVESTA—The collection of sacred texts of Zoroastrians, including hymns (some attributed to Zoroaster himself) and descriptions of religious ceremonies.

AVIDYA—The opposite of *vidya*, meaning knowledge in Indian philosophy, this denotes ignorance in all its forms, emotional and intellectual; misconceptions, misunderstandings, and lack of true self-knowledge.

BODHISATTVA—A saintly person in the Mahayana Buddhist tradition who has taken a compassionate vow to delay final Nirvana until all other sentient beings are saved. Some Bodhisattvas became so revered that they rivaled the Buddha in popularity.

BRAHMAN—"Ultimate reality," "the ground of all being," or "the soul of the universe" in Hinduism. Sometimes translated as "God" in Western literature.

BRAHMIN—A member of the priestly caste in the Indian caste system.

CALVINISM—A major branch of Protestantism that follows the teachings of the French theologian John Calvin (1509–64), who established a Reformed church in Geneva, Switzerland.

DALIT—"Untouchable"; the name that is given to those lower castes who fall outside the four-fold caste system of traditional Hinduism.

DHARMA—The Dharma, meaning "religious practice," is one element of the three jewels (the others being The Buddha and the Samgha) to which Buddhists commit themselves when embarking on the Path. It also has a wider meaning in Hinduism, covering the moral law and order of the universe.

DIASPORA—The dispersion of Jewish communities (often due to persecution) from their traditional homeland, Israel. The term has come to be used of other religious groups who have taken to living away from their roots.

DREAMING, THE—The spiritual realm in Australian Aboriginal religion, relating to the original creation of the land by their ancestors and nature spirits such as the Rainbow Serpent, and accessible today through art, song, and storytelling.

DUKKHA—This Buddhist term is often translated as "suffering." It is the first of the Buddha's Four Noble Truths; his analysis of life being that dis-ease is a fundamental element in life and can only be resolved by recognizing that this teaching is true and following the Buddhist Eightfold Path.

FILIOQUE—(Literally meaning "and the Son.") The creed in the Western Roman Catholic and Protestant churches states that the Holy Spirit comes from God "the Father and the Son." The Orthodox churches believe that it comes only from the Father. This was a theological detail in the great schism that divided Eastern from Western Christendom in the eleventh century.

HADITH—(Meaning "speech" or "report" in Arabic.) The customs, traditions, and practices of the prophet Mohammed, including some of his words, are recorded in the Hadiths. Unlike the Quran, they are not believed to be the direct word of God, but they provided guidance for everyday living for the early Muslim community. Much of *Sharia* law is based upon this collection.

ICON—(Meaning "image" in Greek.) Religious icons in the Christian tradition, usually paintings, typically depicting Jesus Christ, the Virgin Mary, or a saintly figure. They are used devotionally in the Eastern Orthodox churches, both as aids to prayer and through their very creation being in itself an act of worship.

IMMACULATE CONCEPTION—The belief found principally in the Roman Catholic Church that the Virgin Mary was born miraculously without the taint of Original Sin, making her a suitable mother to give birth to Jesus, the Son of God.

INNUA—The invisible forces, good and bad, that control the world according to the Inuit belief system.

JINAS—(Sanskrit for "victory.") The Jain religion venerates 24 *Jinas*, spiritual heroes of the past known as tirthankaras (meaning "ford crossers"), who have been victorious in crossing the stream of rebirths by living a perfect ethical life. They are spiritual role models.

KAMI—Worship of, and respect for, the kami is central to the Shinto religion; they are the spirits and forces of nature; also the genius of certain places, which in English might be referred to as divine or sacred. Some ancestors are seen as kami, as are the spiritual beings in mythology.

KARMA—The moral law in Indian religion that runs throughout life, linking behavior, in thought, word, and deed, to consequences. Bad behavior leads inevitably to suffering in this or the next life; good behavior is eventually rewarded with a spell in paradise or in an advantageous rebirth.

KSHATRIYA—The warrior, ruling caste within Hinduism.

LOTUS SUTRA, THE—(The "Saddharma Pundarika Sutra" in Sanskrit.) One of the most important texts in Mahayana Buddhism, principally in China and Japan, where it became the central scripture for the Nichiren sect.

LUTHERANISM—The collection of theological teachings and churches based upon the work of the German Reformation theologian Martin Luther (1483–1546).

MAHAYANA—Literally "The Greater Vehicle." New forms of Buddhism that developed in China, Japan, and Tibet believed that they offered a superior way of spirituality to that offered by earlier traditions, which they labeled as the Hinayana (the Lesser Vehicle).

MAITREYA—(From a Sanskrit word meaning "loving kindness.") The future Buddha in the Mahayana tradition, currently a Bodhisattva in paradise awaiting rebirth at a time when the world is in need of spiritual guidance.

MANTRA—Sacred words of power used within a religious belief system, chanted repetitively or recited quietly in meditation: they help the mind to focus and to avoid distracting thoughts.

MUDRA—A symbolic hand gesture in Buddhist art.

NIRVANA—(Literally, "blown out" in Sanskrit.) The state of being, beyond words, experienced when fully enlightened in the Buddhist tradition. The illusion of being a separate individual is "blown out" as a candle flame is extinguished.

SAMGHA—The community of monks in Buddhism.

SAMSARA—(Sanskrit for "continuous flowing.") The unending cycle of rebirth, believed by Buddhists, Hindus, and Jains to be the nature of life in this world. The aim of spiritual practice is for the soul to achieve the state of *moksha*—liberation from *Samsara*.

SANDPAINTING—A stylized art form (sometimes called Dry Painting) used in healing ceremonies by Native Americans of the southwestern United States, particularly the Navajo. The pictures, created on the ground from colored sands, are designed to be destroyed to release their healing energy.

SATORI—In Zen Buddhism, the experience of "seeing into one's own nature." It is sometimes translated as "Enlightenment."

SHAMAN—A Siberian Tungusic word referring to a religious type, male or female, found in many cultures worldwide; they are known for being experts in the use of ecstasy in healing ceremonies or supposedly for making journeys into the spirit world.

SHARIA—(Arabic for "way" or "path.") Islamic law based upon the Quran and the Hadith.

SONGLINES—The invisible tracks that criss-cross Australia following the routes taken by the creator-beings who sang the details of the landscape into existence. The remembered songs are part of Aboriginal folklore, providing route maps across the vast expanses of the bush, linking landmarks and waterholes.

TANAKH—A name given to the Jewish Bible, being an acronym of its three sections— Torah (the Law), Neviim (the Prophets), and Ketuvim (the Writings).

THERAVADIN—"The way of the elders"; the early Buddhist tradition labeled by Buddhists of the Mahayana tradition as the Hinayana (the Lesser Vehicle). It survives today principally in Sri Lanka and Thailand.

TRANSUBSTANTIATION—A Christian interpretation, mostly espoused by Roman Catholic theologians, of what happens in Holy Communion (otherwise known as the Eucharist or the Mass): it holds that the bread and wine literally become the body and blood of Jesus Christ, even though their outward appearance remains unchanged.

TWELVERS—The majority within Shi'a Islam who believe in 12 divinely ordained Imams (leaders), the last of which will one day return to the world as the Mahdi, a Messianic figure.

ZAZEN—(Literally, "seated meditation" in Japanese.) The primary practice of meditation in the Zen tradition, details in the method of which vary from school to school.

ZEN—A Japanese school of Mahayana Buddhism that emphasizes the importance of meditation. It is transmitted directly from teacher to pupil and claims to be a tradition outside of the scriptures, focusing on "seeing into one's own nature and the attainment of Buddhahood."

ZOROASTRIANISM—One of the oldest religions in the world based upon the teachings of the Persian prophet Zoroaster (Zarathustra) (approximately sixth century BCE—though some claim he lived much earlier), teaching a dualistic cosmology of good and evil.

ZWINGLIANISM—Huldrych (Ulrich) Zwingli (1484–1531) was a leader of the Reformation in Switzerland based in Zurich. He rejected the Roman Catholic teaching on transubstantiation, arguing that the bread and wine in Holy Communion merely represent the body and blood of Christ. Zwinglianism is the name given to a Reformed confession of faith based on Zwingli's teaching.

FURTHER READING

General

Armstrong, K. *A History of God*. New York: Ballantine Books, 1994.

Cooper, J. C. *An Illustrated Encyclopaedia of Traditional Symbols*. London: Thames and Hudson, 1978.

Gross, A. G. *The Scientific Sublime*. New York: Oxford University Press, 2018.

McGrath, A. *The Great Mystery: Science, God and the Human Quest for Meaning*. London: Hodder and Stoughton, 2017.

McGrath, A. *The Twilight of Atheism: The Rise and Fall of Disbelief in the Modern World*. New York: Doubleday, 2004.

Parrinder, G. *Worship in the World's Religions*. London: Sheldon Press, 1961.

Polkinghorne, J. *Scientists as Theologians*. London: SPCK, 1996.

Rappaport, R. A. *Ritual and Religion in the Making of Humanity*. Cambridge: Cambridge University Press, 1999.

Chapter 1

Doniger, W. (trans). *Hindu Myths*. London: Penguin Classics, 1975.

Mascaro, J. (trans). *The Bhagavad Gita*. London: Penguin Classics, 1962.

Parrinder, G. *Asian Religions*. London: Sheldon Press, 1975.

Radhakrishnan, S. *The Principal Upanishads*. New York: George Allen and Unwin Ltd., 1953.

Rahula, W. *What the Buddha Taught*. Bedford: Gordon Fraser, 1959.

Schumann, H. W. *Buddhism: An Outline of its Teachings and Schools*. London: Rider, 1973.

Sen, K. M. *Hinduism*. London: Penguin Books, 1961.

Smart, N. *The Religious Experience of Mankind*. New York: Charles Scribner's Sons, 1969.

Chapter 2

Bunyan, J. *The Pilgrim's Progress*. London: SPCK, 1947.

Hathout, H. *Reading the Muslim Mind*. Burr Ridge: American Trust Publications, 1995.

Kung, H.; Quinn, E. (trans). *Does God Exist?* New York: Doubleday, 1980.

Maalouf, A. *The Crusades through Arab Eyes*. London: Al Saqi Books, 1984.

Nanji, A. *Dictionary of Islam*. London: Penguin Books, 2008.

Neuberger, J. *Is that all there is? Thoughts on the meaning of Life and Leaving a Legacy*. London: Rider, 2011.

Neuberger, J. *On Being Jewish*. London: Heinemann, 1995.

Sanders, N. K. *The Epic of Gilgamesh*. London: Penguin Classics, 1960.

Shah, I. *The Way of the Sufi*. New York: Dutton, 1969.

Spong, J. S. *A New Christianity for a New World*. San Francisco: HarperSanFrancisco, 2002.

Vermes, G. *Jesus the Jew: A Historian's Reading of the Gospels*. London: William Collins, 1973.

Chapter 3

Anesaki, M. *History of Japanese Religion*. Rutland, Vt.: Charles E. Tuttle, 1963.

Blofeld, J. *Compassion Yoga: The Mystical Cult of Kuan Yin*. London: Mandala Books, 1977.

Chan, W. et al. *The Great Asian Religions: An Anthology*. New York: Macmillan, 1969.

Jordan, D. K. *Gods, Ghosts and Ancestors: Folk Religion in a Taiwanese Village*. Berkeley: University of California Press, 1972.

Soothill, W. E. (trans). *The Analects of Confucius*. Oxford: Oxford University, 1962.

Tzu, L.; Lau, D.C. (trans). *Tao Te Ching*. London: Penguin Classics, 1963.

Watts, A. *Tao: The Watercourse Way*. London: Pelican Books, 1979.

Watts, A. *The Way of Zen*. New York: Vintage Books, 1989.

Wilhelm, R. (trans.) *The I Ching: The Book of Changes*. London: Routledge and Kegan Paul, 1968.

Chapter 4

Barker, E. *New Religious Movements: A Practical Introduction*. London: HMSO Publications, 1989.

Batchelor, M. and Brown, K. (eds) *Buddhism and Ecology*. London: Cassell in association with the World Wide Fund for Nature, 1992.

Breuilly E. and Palmer M. (eds) *Christianity and Ecology*. London: Cassell in association with the World Wide Fund for Nature, 1992.

Campbell, J. *Myths to Live By*. New York: Viking Press, 1972.

Chatwin, B. *The Songlines*. New York: Penguin Books, 2012.

Eliade, M. *Shamanism: Archaic Techniques of Ecstasy*. New York: Pantheon Books, 1964.

Evans, C. *Cults of Unreason*. London: George G. Harrap and Co. Ltd., 1973.

Khalid, F. with O'Brien, J. (eds) *Islam and Ecology*. London: Cassell in association with the World Wide Fund for Nature, 1992.

Lewis, J. R. (ed.) *The Gods Have Landed: New Religions from Other Worlds*. Albany: State University of New York Press, 1995.

Neihardt, J. G. *Black Elk Speaks*. New York: Pocket Books, 1972.

Newcomb, F. J. and Reichard, G. A. *Sandpaintings of the Navajo Shooting Chant*. New York: Dover Publications, 1975.

Prime, R. *Hinduism and Ecology*. London: Cassell in association with the World Wide Fund for Nature, 1992.

Rose, A. (ed.) *Judaism and Ecology*. London: Cassell in association with the World Wide Fund for Nature, 1992.

Ryan, J. *Mythscapes: Aboriginal Art of the Desert*. Exhibition catalogue. Melbourne: National Gallery of Victoria, 1989.

Thomas, R. *I Want to Paint*. Exhibition catalogue, East Perth: Heylesbury Pty Ltd, 2003.

INDEX

A

Aboriginal religion 119, 124–125
Abraham 48
Abu Bakr 53, 72
advaita 18
Aetherius Society 138
Aga Khan IV 76
Agni 18
ahimsa 15, 17, 38, 39
Ahriman, Lord of Darkness 42
Ahura Mazda 42
Ali 72, 74
Allat 56
Amaterasu 87, 98, 100
Amitabha 34, 83, 92, 93, 105
Amos 57
Analects 82, 86, 88
anatta 34
ancestor worship 82, 96–97, 122, 124
Angad, Guru 19
Anglicanism 61, 62, 64–65
Apasmara 37
Apostles' Creed 58
Applewhite, Marshall 139
Arjan, Guru 44
Arjuna 28
Assassins, the 77
atman 18
Augustine, St. 64
Avalokiteśvara 104, 105
Avesta, the 42
avidya 37
Ayers Rock *see* Uluru
Aztecs 120, 128–129

B

Bab 78, 79
Baha'i faith 78–79
Bahá'u'lláh 78, 79
Baptists 62, 70–71
Bardo, the 97
Barlaam 52
Bhagavad Gita 21, 28

bhakti 20, 21, 92
birdman cult, Easter Island 110
Black Elk 119, 137
Bodhidharma 94
bodhisattvas 34, 35, 83
Book of Common Prayer, The 61, 64, 65
Book of Psalms 52
Book of Revelation 53
Brahma 26, 30
Brahman 20, 21, 26
Brahmins, the 22, 23
Buddha, the 15, 16, 24, 32, 33, 35, 36, 37, 113
Buddhism 24, 32–33, 83
   Hinayana 34
   Mahayana 34–35, 83, 92, 97, 105
   Pure Land 92–93
   Theravada 34
   Zen 83, 94–95
   see also mandalas; Mara the Evil One; Nichiren; Pali canon
Bunyan, John: *The Pilgrim's Progress* 71

C

Cadbury, George 68
Calvinism 62
cargo cults, Melanesia 112–113
caste system 22–23
Catholicism 60–61
Chicomecohuatl 129
Ch'in Shih Huang, Emperor 86
Christianity 43, 49, 58–59, 117
   see also Jesus Christ; Mary, the Virgin and individual branches and texts
Chuang Tzu 85
Chukwu 116

Church of England 64
Church of Jesus Christ of Latter Day Saints *see* Mormons
Confucianism 82, 88–89
Confucius 82, 86, 88
Cook, James 126
Cortés, Hernán 120, 128
Cranmer, Thomas 65
cult heroes 113

D

Dalits 22, 23
Decalogue *see* Ten Commandments
dharma 29
Diamond Sutra 35
Dreamtime 119, 124–125
Dual (Ryobu) Shinto 100–101
dukkha 32

E

Easter Island 110–111
Eastern Orthodox churches 61, 66–67
ecology 146–147
Edinburgh, Prince Philip, Duke of 113
Eightfold Path 32
Epic of Gilgamesh, The 31
Esu 123
Ezekiel 56

F

False Face Society 117
Falun Gong 106–107
Fatimah 74, 76
filioque 66, 67
flood stories 30–31
Florentine Codex 120
Four Noble Truths 32
Fox, George 68
Francis of Assisi, St. 147
Frum, John 112
Fry, Elizabeth 68

G

Gaia 146, 147
Gandhi, Mahatma 17, 38
Ganesha 27
Garvey, Marcus 118, 140
Gathas, the 43
Gautama, Siddhartha *see* Buddha, the
Al Ghazzali 75
Ghost Dance 136
Ginsberg, Alan 95
glossolalia see speaking in tongues
Gobind Singh 19
Gohonzon of Nichiren 109
Golden Rule 86
Golden Temple, Amritsar 44
Guru Granth Sahib 19, 44

H

Hadiths 72
haiku 95
Haile Selassie, Emperor 118, 140
Hajj 72
Hallaj 75
Hanuman 27
Hassan-i Sabbah 77
Heaven's Gate 139
Henry VIII, King 65
Hildegard of Bingen, St. 50
Hinayana Buddhism 34
Hinduism 14, 20–21, 24, 37
  caste system 22–23
  flood story 30
  gods 26–27
  see also Bhagavad Gita; *Mahabharata*; *Manusmriti*
Huitzilopochtli 128
Husayn 74

I

I-Ching 89
Ibn Arabi 75
icons 66

Imams 74
Indra 18
Innua 134
Inuit religion 134–135
Isaiah 56
Ishmael 48
Islam 49, 72–73
  Shi'a Islam 74–75
  Sunni Islam 74, 76
  see also Mohammed; Quran
Ismailism 76–77
Izanagi 87
Izanami 87

J

Jade Emperor 91
Jainism 15, 24, 38–39
Jatis 22
Jeremiah 56
Jesus Christ 49, 53, 56, 58, 60, 61, 113
Jesus Prayer, the 41
Jibreel (Gabriel) 51
Jihad 76
Jinus 38
John, St. 53, 58
John the Divine, St. 53
Josaphat 52
Judaism 48–49, 54–55
Jung, Carl G. 109
"justification by faith" 62, 63

K

Kabir 16
Kali 26
kami 83, 87, 98
karma 20, 24, 38
Kerouac, Jack 95
Khadija 51
King, George 138
King, Martin Luther 38, 118
Kings, First Book of 120–121
koans 94
Kojiki 83, 87
Krishna, Lord 28

Kshatriyas, the 22
Kurirr, the 119
Kwannon 104–105

L

Lang, D. M. 52
Lao Tzu 82–83, 90, 91
Lehna, Guru 16
Li Hongzhi 106
Lotus of the True Law 35
Lotus Sutra 85, 105, 108, 109
Lovelock, James 147
Luke, St. 53
Luther, Martin 62, 63

M

Ma-tsu 84
Mahabharata 20, 22, 28–29, 30
Maharishi Mahesh Yogi 40
Mahavira (Vardhamana) 15, 38
Mahayana Buddhism 34–35, 83, 92, 97, 105
Mahdi, the 74
Maitreya 34
Make-make 110
Manat 56
mandalas 109
mantras 40, 41
Manu 19, 30
Manusmriti 19
Māori religion 126–127
Mara the Evil One 36–37
Maranatha 41
Mark, St. 53
Marley, Bob 141
Mary, the Virgin 51
Matthew, St. 53
Maui 127
Melanesian cargo cults 112–113
Mencius 84
Micah 57
Miki, Nakayama 102

Mindfulness 33
missionary religions 117
Moai, Easter Island 111
Mohammed 49, 51, 56, 72, 75, 113
moksha 19, 20, 38
Mormons 117, 142–143
mudras 93

N
Nanak, Guru 15, 16, 19, 44
natural world, veneration of 116–117
  see also ecology
Navajo religion 132–133
  sandpaintings 121, 133
Nazri Ismailis 76
nembutsu, the 92
Nero, Emperor 53
Nettles, Bonnie 139
New Testament, The 53
Newcomb, Franc J. 121
Nicene Creed 58, 60
Nichiren 85, 108
Nihongi 83, 87
Nirvana 32, 34, 92
Noah 31

O
Odin 130
Olorun 116–117, 122, 123
Om 18, 40
Origen 25
Orisa, the 122
Orpheus 130, 131

P
Pali canon 18
Parsees 15, 43
Parvati 27
Passover, the 54
Paul, St. 53, 59
Penn, William 68
Pentecostalism 117, 144–145
Peter, St. 53, 60

Pilgrim's Progress, The (Bunyan) 71
Plato 25
Popes 60
Prabhutaratna 109
Presbyterian church 62
prophets 56–57
Protestantism 62–63
psalms 65
Pure Land Buddhism 92–93
Pythagoras 25

Q
Quakers 68–69
Quetzalcoatl 128
Quran 51, 53, 56, 72

R
Ramayana 20, 29
Rastafarians 117, 118, 120, 140–141
Reichard, Gladys A. 121
reincarnation 14, 20, 24–25, 38, 97
Rig Veda 18
Roman Catholic Church 60–61
rosaries 41
Rowntree, Joseph 68

S
sacraments 61
Sahagún, Bernardino de 120, 129
Sakyamuni 85, 109
salah 72
Samsara 24, 38
sandpaintings 121, 133
Satan 37
"Satanic Verses, The" 56
Satapatha Brahmana 30
satori 94
sawm 72
Scivias, the 50
Sedna 134–135

shahada 72
shaktis 26
Shamanism 130–131, 134
Sharia law 72, 73
Sheba, Queen of 120, 140
Shi'a Islam 74–75
Shinto 83, 87, 98–9
  Dual (Ryobu) Shinto 100–101
  State Shinto 101
Shiva 20, 26, 27, 37
Shudras, the 22
Sikhism 15, 16, 19, 44–45
Sleipnir 130
Smith, Joseph, II 142
Smyth, John 70
Society of Friends 68–69
Soka Gakkai International 108–109
Solomon, King 120–121, 140
Songlines 124
Space Age Cults 138–139
speaking in tongues 144, 145
State Shinto 101
sufis 75
Sun Dance 137
Sunni Islam 74, 76
Susanoo 87, 98
Suzuki, D. T. 95

T
Taekwondo 107
Tai chi 107
Tanakh, the 48, 55
Tangata manu birdman cult 110
Tao Te Ching 82–83, 90, 91
Taoism 90–91
tapu 126
Tawhid 76
Ten Commandments 55, 121
Tenri-kyo 102–103
Teresa, Mother 17
Tezcatlipoca 128
Theravada Buddhism 34

Thomas, Rover 119
Thummim 142
Tien 88
Tipitaka, the 18
Tlaloc 128
Torah, the 55
Torii arches 99
Transcendental Meditation
40–41
transubstantiation 61
Trinity, doctrine of the 66
Tseng 86
Twelvers 74, 76

U
Uluru 124, 125
untouchables 22, 23
Upanishads 18

Urim 142
Uzzar 56

V
Vairocana 100
Vaishnavism 26
Vaishyas, the 22
Vedanta, the 19, 40
Vishnu 20, 26, 30
Vyasa 29

W
Waheguru 45
Wakan Tanka 116
Watts, Alan 95
Whirling Dervishes 75
"Wisdom of Balahvar, The" 52

Wovoka 136
wu-wei 90

Y
yin and *yang* 85, 89
yoga 21
Yoruba religion 117, 122–123
Young, Brigham 143
Yu 86
Yudhishthira, King 29

Z
zakat 72
zazen 94
Zen Buddhism 83, 94–95
Zoroastrianism 15, 42–43
Zwinglianism 62

ABOUT THE AUTHOR

Adam Ford is an ordained Anglican priest, now retired. He was formerly Priest-in-Ordinary to Her Majesty the Queen at the Chapel Royal, chaplain to a London school, and vicar of a Yorkshire town. He has an MA in Indian religions and has often lectured on Buddhism, Hinduism, and astronomy. He is the author of five books on mindfulness, including *The Art of Mindful Walking* (2012) and *The Art of Mindful Silence* (2011); and several books for children, both fiction (such as *The Cuckoo Plant*—1991) and non-fiction (*Stars: a Family Guide to the Night Sky*—2015). A lifelong interest has been in the relationship between religion and science, about which he has written extensively. Adam has four children and seven grandchildren, is married to Ros Roscoe, and lives in the UK in East Sussex.

ACKNOWLEDGMENTS

My grateful thanks to the team at Ivy Press, Tom Kitch, Susan Kelly, Caroline Earle, Claire Saunders, and Nick Fawcett, who have supported me with invaluable help and encouragement in the writing of this book.

Picture credits